THE BEST OF
POLISH
COOKING

Recipes for Entertaining
and Special Occasions

by
Karen West

HIPPOCRENE BOOKS
New York, New York

Library of Congress Cataloging in Publication Data

West, Karen.
  The best of Polish cooking.

  1. Cookery, Polish.   I. Title.
TX723.5.P6W7 1983   641.59438   83-48632
ISBN 0-87052-787-8

Hippocrene Books paperback edition, 1989

Printed in the United States of America

Contents

Introduction	7
Spring Menus	9
Summer Menus	73
Autumn Menus	107
Winter Menus	141
Vodka	179
Index	195

This book is dedicated to my husband, Louis, who has stoically sampled *all* my experimental recipes. Those he enjoyed, you will find on the following pages.

K.W.

Introduction

Polish food seems made for hospitality. It is a cuisine that features perfect, fresh ingredients of the season and abounds with recipes for wonderful hors d'oeuvre, fragrant soups, and delicate sausages. Many flavorings are used—most especially onion and fresh dill—but always with a light hand. Polish cooks take pride in being subtle and their food shows this skill and care.

This is food that is perfectly suited to entertaining: it is delicious, unusual, and is mostly prepared ahead of time so that the host or hostess can enjoy the party as much as the guests. Menus are given here to let you explore the delights of Polish food while following the cycle of the seasons because the freshest foods in season are best—and usually the most economical as well.

So, plan a party, ask your friends over, and have a wonderful time.

Karen West

Spring
Menus

No season is as joyfully anticipated as Spring. There are vernal pleasures to titillate every sense, but the greatest pleasures await the palate. Now one can find the tenderest asparagus tips, the freshest rhubarb stalks. Enjoy delicate spring lamb and celebrate with the first red strawberries of the season.

What could be more appropriate to celebrate Spring's arrival than garden-fresh young vegetables made into soup with dumplings and a spring chicken? Choose one of the following recipes for barshch, and serve a festive dessert such as Mazurka Royale for a truly inspired meal.

SPRING MENU FOR 4

Spring Barshch / Barszcz Wiosenny
(or one of the Special Soup Recipes)
Lettuce and Sliced Eggs Salad / Sałata z Jajkami
Chicken Paprika / Paprykarz z Kury
New Potato Dumplings / Knedelki z Kartoli
Masurka Royale / Muzurek Królewski

SPECIAL SOUP RECIPES

Homemade Chicken Stock / Rosół Domowy z Kury
Beet Soup / Zupa Buraczana
Clear Beet Soup / Cienka Zupa Buraczana
Cold Beet Soup with Beet Greens /
Zupa z Liści Burakowych na Zimno
Easy Barshch / Lekki Barszcz
Beetroot Soup / Barszcz Czerwony
Basic Beef Broth / Rosół Wołowy
Hot Beer Barshch / Goracy Barszcz na Piwie
Hot Beer Soup / Zupa z Piwa na Goraco

Barszcz may be served hot or cold; clear or thick; with vegetables, with or without meat; as an appetizer or as a meal, but, it must be served always, *always*, with sour cream.

Spring Barshch

Barszcz Wiosenny

3 bunches young beets, washed and chopped
3 cups water
2 tablespoons lemon juice
6 cups chicken stock OR
    6 cups water and 6 bouillon cubes*
3 tablespoons flour
½ cup water
salt to taste
3 teaspoons dill
3 teaspoons chopped parsley
1 finely chopped onion
2 tablespoons butter
1 cup sour cream
3 quartered hard-cooked eggs

Simmer beets with the lemon juice in water for ½ hour. Add the broth and the flour/water mixutre. Simmer while stirring continuously for 10 minutes. Season with salt, herbs and butter. Serve garnished with sour cream and sieved or riced, hard-cooked egg yolks.

Note Hard-cook enough eggs for both the barshch and the Lettuce and Sliced Egg Salad.

*Bouillon cubes and water, or canned broth, work just as well as your own broth, but are much faster. The following recipe for chicken stock is for the purists.

Homemade Chicken Stock
Rosół Domowy z Kury

1 *whole chicken* OR *3 pounds necks and wings*
3 *tablespoons lemon juice*
3 *onions, each stuck with a whole clove*
4 *stalks celery*
4 *scallions, sliced*
2 *carrots, sliced*
3 *tablespoons chopped parsley*
⅛ *teaspoon thyme*
2 *bay leaves*
salt to taste
4 *peppercorns*
2 *quarts water*

Baste meat with lemon juice. Place in kettle and cover with water. Bring to a boil, then skim. Add the rest of the ingredients and simmer for 2½ hours, or until meat is tender. Remove the chicken; put meat aside for another use and replace the bones and skin in stock. Simmer for 45 minutes. Strain through a sieve or cheesecloth. Chill and skim fat from the top.

Beet Soup
Zupa Buraczana

½ *cup dried lima beans*
8 *beets, peeled and quartered*
1 *cup stewing beef, cubed*
soup bone (optional)
1 *cup stewed tomatoes*
12 *cups water*
1 *head cabbage, shredded*
1 *apple, peeled and quartered*
salt and pepper to taste
½ *cup sour cream*

Soak beans overnight. Cook in the same water for 2 hours and drain, then set aside. Mix beets, beef, tomatoes and water. Bring to a boil, then skim. Simmer for 1½ hours. Add the cabbage, apple, salt, pepper, and bone, then simmer for another hour. Remove and grind the beets, then return to the soup. Mix with the beans. Serve with sour cream.

Clear Beet Soup
Cienka Zupa Buraczana

2 cups beets, peeled and shredded
1 pound shank beef
2 soup bones
2 quarts water
1 cup diced celery
salt to taste
4 peppercorns
2 chopped onions
1 bay leaf
1 teaspoon allspice
2 crushed cloves garlic
2 tablespoons honey
1 cup sour beet juice (optional)
½ cup sour cream

Simmer beets until tender, about 15 minutes. Drain and put aside the liquid. (Use the beets for another dish.) Boil the meat, bones and water, then simmer for ½ hour. Add the vegatables and spices; simmer until the meat is done. Strain; set meat aside. Add the juices to the sour beet juice and 1 cup of the water the beets were cooked in. Heat to the boiling point. If desired, garnish with sour cream. (An excellent accompaniment to this soup is stuffed dumplings or potatoes.)

Cold Beet Soup with Beet Greens
Zupa z Liści Burakowych ňa Zimno

1½ pounds veal with bone
2 quarts cold water
1 cup sliced celery
½ cup grated carrot
2 cloves garlic
1 bay leaf
6 large shrimp OR
 6 crayfish
1 cup beets with greens
1 cup dill pickle juice
3 coarsely chopped hard-cooked eggs
1 teaspoon chopped, fresh dill
1 chopped cucumber
3 tablespoons flour
1½ cups sour cream
salt and pepper to taste
2 tablespoons sugar

Combine the veal and water; bring to a boil, then simmer for ½ hour. Add the celery, carrots, garlic and bay leaf and simmer for ½ hour more Clean the shrimp (if using crayfish be sure to scour WELL) and simmer in a separate pan for 10 minutes. Peel and shred the beets and greens; simmer until tender with veal and vegetable mixture. Shell the fish, dice, and add to soup. Add the chopped eggs, dill and cucumber.

Remove the meat from the stock and dice Remove the bay leaf and discard. Mix sour cream with the flour and add to stock with the pickle juice. Bring to a boil; add veal and simmer for 5 minutes. Combine remaining ingredients with the mixture. Chill and serve with extra sour cream for a garnish.

Easy Barshch
Lekki Barszcz

3 cups beef stock (either home-made or canned)
½ cabbage, chopped
3 beets, peeled and cubed OR
    1 1-lb. can beets
½ lemon, sliced
3 chopped onions
1 sprig fresh dill, chopped
1 potato, peeled and cubed
1½ cups sour cream

Place all ingredients, but sour cream, into a kettle and simmer for 45 minutes, or until vegetables are tender. Remove the lemon. After soup has cooled a bit, add the sour cream.

Beetroot Soup
Barszcz Czerwony

3 strips crumbled bacon
1 sliced leek
1 onion, thinly sliced
1½ cups shredded cabbage
2 raw beetroots, slivered
½ cup sour cream (optional)
1 tablespoon tomato paste
6 cups beef stock
2 tablespoons wine vinegar
salt to taste
3 peppercorns

Sauté the bacon slowly with the leek and onion until golden. Add the rest of the ingredients and bring to a boil. Simmer for 1 hour. Garnish with sour cream.

Basic Beef Broth

Rosół Wołowy

1½ pounds shin bone and knuckle
1½ pounds beef rump, cut into 1-inch cubes
4 quarts water
salt to taste
10 peppercorns
3 bay leaves
3 sliced onions
2 carrots, cut in chunks
4 sprigs parsley
1 white turnip, cubed
dash thyme
3 whole cloves

Have the butcher crack the knuckle and shinbone. Place the bones and meat in a large kettle and cover with water. Add the remaining ingredients and bring to a boil. Simmer for 3 hours. Skim several times. Remove the meat and use for another purpose. Strain the broth through a sieve or cheesecloth. Remove the fat from the top when chilled.

The Polish are very fond of beer; they immeasurably prefer it to wine in their cooking. Kvas, a fermented drink, is called for in this next recipe. It is heavier than U.S. domestic beers, but similar to German varieties.

Unless you live near a neighborhood store that imports it, Kvas is very difficult to locate. Either domestic or German beer may be substituted.

Hot Beer Barshch
Gorący Barszcz na Piwie

1 pound raw, sliced beetroot
4 cups water
½ cup rye bread crusts
2 cups Kvas
2 cups water or beef stock
½ cup sour cream

Place beetroot in a large bowl. Boil the 4 cups of water, allow to cool, then pour over the beetroot. Add the rye crusts and cover the mixture with a clean cloth. Leave in a warm spot, untouched for 3 to 4 days, or until the beetroot begins to ferment. (The time can vary according to taste.) Combine this with the Kvas and stock, then heat. Serve with sour cream.

Hot Beer Soup
Zupa z Piwa na Gorąco

4 cups beer
4 cups water
2 tablespoons sugar
1 tablespoon butter
3 egg yolks
1 cup heavy cream

Mix the beer with the water and bring to a boil; stir in the sugar and butter, then simmer for ½ hour. Beat egg yolks until frothy. Add the cream to the yolks and beat again. Gradually fold the beer mixture into the egg-cream, beating continuously. Simmer the soup for another 10 minutes. (To avoid curdling do NOT bring to a boil.) Serve in preheated bowls.

Fresh green salads are not as popular in Poland as they are here, however there are a variety of salads that are uniquely Polish. Onion, cabbage, sauerkraut, leek and apple are some of the more favored ingredients used in these salads. Lemon juice and sour cream are usually used for the dressing, but mayonnaise may be substituted.

Lettuce and Sliced Egg Salad
Saɫata z Jajkami

2 heads lettuce, washed
1 cup sour cream
dash salt
1 teaspoon honey
6 sliced hard-cooked eggs OR
  6 sliced, pickled eggs (see index)
1 sliced onion

Separate lettuce leaves and arrange on platter. Mix the dressing of the sour cream, salt and honey and pour over the lettuce. Arrange the sliced eggs and sliced onion on top. Chill and serve.

Chicken Paprika
Papprykarz z Kury

4 chicken breasts, with wings
4 tablespoons butter
1 diced onion
2 large tomatoes, peeled
1 small diced green pepper
dash salt
¼ cup water
½ cup sour cream
2 tablespoons flour

Lightly brown the chicken in the butter and remove. Sauté the onions in the same skillet. Add all ingredients except the sour cream and flour. Blend the sour cream with the flour and slowly add it to the rest of the ingredients. Simmer for 20 minutes and serve.

New Potato Dumplings
Knedelki z Kartoli

6 boiled potatoes, peeled and riced
3 tablespoons finely chopped parsley
1 cup flour
3 eggs
½ cup bacon bits and drippings

Mix all ingredients except bacon. Form small balls with your hands, then drop the dumpling balls in a large kettle of boiling water for about 5 minutes, or until they rise to the top of the water. Cook only a few at a time. Remove the dumplings with a slotted spoon. Keep completed dumplings warm until all are cooked, then drizzle the bacon bits and drippings over the dumplings just before serving.

Mazurkas are traditionally only served on Easter, but with the infinite variety of recipes available it seems foolish not to bake these delicacies at other times of the year as well.

Mazurka Royale
Mazurek Królewski

1 cup butter
1 cup plus 2 tablespoons sugar
8 ounces ground almonds
1 teaspoon vanilla extract
1 orange rind, grated
6 egg whites
1½ cups flour, sifted

Thoroughly cream the butter and sugar. Combine with the almonds, vanilla and orange rind.

Beat the egg whites until stiff. Alternately add the flour and the egg whites to the mixture.

Roll out thin and place on a buttered cookie sheet. Spread dough with fingers to cover sheet entirely. Bake at 350°F for 35 minutes. Cool slightly, then cut into "diamond" squares.

Note: Save the egg yolks for Bechamel Sauce or other recipes.

SPRING LUNCHEON FOR 4

Apples in Creamy Beet Glaze /
Jabłka w Glazurze Buraczanej
Dutch Oven Braised Ham / Szynka Duszona w Rondlu
Eggs with Bechamel Sauce / Jaja Sadzone w Białym Sosie
Black Poppy Seed Rolls / Bułeczki z Makiem
Asparagus au Gratin / Szparagi Wypiekane z Tarta Bułeczką
Almond Baba / Babka Migdałowa

Apples are a favorite relish for ham. Here's an unusual way of serving both as an accompaniment for the Eggs with Bechamel Sauce. The verdant asparagus and the fresh ham are perfect choices for a Spring party.

Apples in Creamy Beet Glaze

Jabłka w Glazurze Buraczanej

1 *pound cooked beets, drained and minced,* OR
  1 1-lb. can beets, drained and minced
3 *tablespoons beet juice*
2 *tablespoons flour or cornstarch, which makes a
  more transparent glaze*
salt to taste
1 *teaspoon sugar*
2 *apples, peeled, cored and diced*
½ *cup sour cream*
1 *tablespoon lemon juice*

Gently warm the beets. Mix the beet juice with the flour (or cornstarch) and add to the beets along with the salt and sugar. Bring to a boil. Stir in remaining ingredients. Keep warm, but do not boil.

Dutch Oven Braised Ham

Szynka Duszona w Rondlu

1 *2-lb. slice fresh ham*
2 *tablespoons flour*
3 *tablespoons bacon drippings* OR
  3 tablespoons butter
¼ *cup broth* OR
  water
2 *sliced onions*
2 *teaspoons caraway seeds*

Dredge ham with the flour and lightly brown in the drippings with the onions. Add the rest of the ingredients and simmer for 1½ hours.

Eggs with Bechamel Sauce
Jaja Sadzone w Białym Sosie

8 hard-cooked eggs
1 raw egg, beaten
½ cup bread crumbs
¼ cup butter

Cool and shell the hard-cooked eggs. Dip each peeled whole egg into the raw egg and then roll in the bread crumbs. Sauté gently in the butter until warmed through. Place on a heated platter and dress with the Bechamel Sauce.
Note: Use half the Bechamel Sauce recipe for the eggs, and the other half for the asparagus.

Bechamel Sauce

4 tablespoons butter
4 tablespoons flour
2 cups milk
dash salt
½ teaspoon lemon juice
6 egg yolks (use the leftover yolks from the Mazurka Royale)

Make a roux of the butter and flour. Gradually add the milk, while stirring continuously. Remove from heat.
   Mix 3 tablespoons of the sauce with the other ingredients, then combine yolk mixture with the rest of the sauce. Heat over medium heat for about 5 minutes, or until thickened.
Note: To use only a small amount of juice from a fresh lemon without wasting the rest of it, roll a lemon across the countertop several times. Then, prick it with a fork

and squeeze out the desired amount of juice. The lemon remains almost intact and can be used again for other purposes.

Asparagus au Gratin

Szparagi Wypiekane z Tarta Bułeczką

2 pounds asparagus
salted water
Bechamel Sauce
4 tablespoons cheese, grated
3 tablespoons buttered bread crumbs

Wash asparagus; scrub gently with a vegetable brush. Cook whole, just barely covered in boiling, salted water for 10 to 15 minutes. Drain and arrange in a flat baking dish. Cover with the Bechamel Sauce. Sprinkle with cheese and bread crumbs and lightly brown under the broiler until the sauce is bubbly.

Almond Baba

Babka Migdałowa

1 cup sugar
10 eggs, separated
1½ cups ground almonds
juice of 1 lemon
2 cups flour (potato flour is best)

Cream the sugar with the egg yolks until frothy and lemon colored. Add the ground almonds and juice and mix well. Beat the egg whites until stiff, then fold into the almond mixture alternately with sifted flour. Pour into a greased mold and bake at 450°F for 30 minutes.

SPRING BRUNCH FOR 4

Spring Cream Cheese Spread /
Wiosenna Przyprawa z Sera Śmietankowego
Freshly Baked Potato Bread / Świeży Chleb Kartoflany
Eggs Sunny Side Up / Sadzone Oczkà z Jajek
Kielbasa / Kiełbasa
Homemade Kielbasa / Kiełbasa Domowa
Savoy Cabbage Polonaise / Kapusta Włoska po Polsku
Wild Strawberries with Whipped Sour Cream /
Poziomki z Bitą Śmietaną

This basic sausage-and-egg meal is given distinction by virtue of the Spring Cream Cheese Spread on Freshly Baked Potato Bread and the delightful wild strawberries.

Spring Cream Cheese Spread
Wiosenna Przyprawa z Sera Smietankowego

½ cup sour cream
1 cup cottage cheese
salt to taste
1 peeled and sliced cucumber
2 tablespoons chopped green onion
lettuce leaves
6 radishes, sliced

Beat the sour cream and cottage cheese until blended. In a separate bowl salt the sliced cucumber and drain. Combine the cucumber with the cheese mixture and chopped onion. Arrange on lettuce leaves. Garnish with the sliced radishes, and serve with homemade potato bread.

Freshly Baked Potato Bread
Świezy Chleb Kartoflany

1 package active dry yeast
¼ cup potato cooking water*
2½ cups potato cooking water*
1 cup cooked and mashed potatoes*
2 tablespoons butter
2 tablespoons sugar
1 teaspoon salt
6 cups flour, sifted
*reserve these items from a prior day's mashed
    potatoes

Soften the yeast in the warmed ¼ cup potato water. Mix the other 2½ cups potato water with the mashed potatoes, butter, sugar, and salt. Blend well. Add half of the flour while beating continuously. Add the yeast, then stir in the remaining flour. Knead the dough on a floured board until smooth.

Put dough in a greased container; butter top of dough and cover. Let it rise in a warm spot until doubled in bulk. Punch it down and divide in half. Shape into 2 loaves and place in buttered bread pans. Cover again and let rise until double in volume. Bake at 375° for 35 to 40 minutes.

Kielbasa

Kiełbasa

1 sausage ring
water to cover
½ cup chopped shallots
2 tablespoons butter

Pierce the sausage casing with a fork to prevent its splitting. Simmer the sausage for 30 minutes in water to cover, then drain, and sauté with the shallots and the butter until the shallots brown lightly.

Making sausages is one of the oldest methods of preparing and preserving meat. As early as 1500 BC the Babylonians were already mastering the art. Rome thought so highly of sausage that it was *de rigueur* to serve it at every feast and banquet. Sausages were so often a part of the menus at infamous orgies that finally they were forbidden, along with the decadent Roman life style, by later reformers. The prohibition only served to make the sausages more desirable to the people.

After the Crusades, when Europe first tasted Eastern spices, all sorts of new recipes for new flavors of sausage were devised. Eventually each nationality refined its own tastes. Following is a recipe for homemade Polish sausage.

Homemade Kielbasa
Kiełbasa Domowa

> *3 pounds raw pork shoulder, chopped, or coarsely*
>   *ground*
> *¾ pound raw beef chuck, coarsely ground*
> *sausage casings*
> *1 tablespoon salt*
> *½ teaspoon pepper OR to taste*
> *¼ teaspoon marjoram*
> *3 cloves garlic, chopped*
> *2 teaspoons honey*

Combine all the ingredients except casings, and mix well. Sauté until well done and stuff into casings, forming foot-long links. Refrigerate for 4 days to cure.

Savoy Cabbage Polonaise
Kapusta Włoska po Polsku

> *1 medium-sized Savoy cabbage*
> *salt to taste*
> *water to cover cabbage*
> *3 tablespoons butter*
> *3 tablespoons dried bread crumbs*

Remove the wilted leaves of the cabbage and cut into 6 to 8 wedges. Cook uncovered in the salted, boiling water for 10 to 15 minutes. Drain. Melt the butter over low heat, and brown the bread crumbs in it. Drizzle the sautéed bread crumbs over the top of the cabbage wedges.

Wild Strawberries with Whipped Sour Cream

Poziomki z Bitą Smietanąą

½ cup vanilla sugar
2 pints wild strawberries
2 cups sour cream

Whip the vanilla sugar and sour cream with an electric mixer as if whipping sweet cream. Gently wash and hull the berries. Serve the cream over the wild strawberries.

Vanilla Sugar

Insert one vanilla bean into each pound of sugar. Let stand for two weeks in an airtight container.

SPRING BRUNCH FOR 4

Fresh Celery Root Salad / Sałatka z Korzeni Selerowych
Celery Vinegar I / Ocet Selerowy
Bulls Eye Eggs / Wole Oczka z Jajek
Braised Liver with Bacon / Wątroba Duszona z Wędzonką
Cabbage Stuffed Pierogi / Pierożki z Kapusty
Baby Carrots Polonaise / Młoda Marchewka po Polsku
Cracklings / Chrusty

Here's hearty fare for brisk, early Spring. Invite several guests over for a warm visit and enough good food to tackle the chilliest of March days!

Fresh Celery Root Salad
Sałatka z Korzeni Selerowych

4 celery roots, cleaned, pared and diced
3 apples, pared, cored and diced
salt and pepper to taste
½ cup olive oil
⅓ cup celery vinegar

Combine all ingredients, lightly toss, and chill for several hours. Serves 4.
Note: Other vinegar may be substituted.

Celery Vinegar
Ocet Selerowy

Boil a quart of white vinegar with 10 peppercorns, 1 teaspoon salt and 4 cups of finely chopped young celery roots for 3 minutes. Pour mixture into sterilized glass bottles, seal and let steep for about 4 weeks. Then strain, and pour into a decanter.

Bulls Eye Eggs
Wole Oczka z Jajek

4 eggs
4 slices French bread
2 tablespoons butter
½ cup heavy cream
lettuce leaves
4 anchovy fillets

Remove centers from bread and sauté crusts in butter. Pour half the cream in the bottom of a baking dish.

Arrange the bread crusts. Break an egg into each crust. Pour the remaining cream evenly over eggs. Bake at 350°F for about 15 minutes. Serve in lettuce cups with an anchovy over each egg.

Braised Liver with Bacon
Wątroba Duszona z Wędzonką

4 slices bacon
4 tablespoons bacon fat
1½ pounds calf's liver, cut into ½-inch slices
1 cup milk
½ cup flour
salt and pepper to taste

Fry (do not broil) the bacon until it is crisp. Reserve the bacon fat and crumble the bacon into bits. Allow the liver to soak in milk for 3 hours. Remove any membranes. (Snip out the veins with kitchen scissors.) Dredge the liver slices in the seasoned flour and brown quickly on both sides in the bacon fat. Liver should not be overcooked; 5 to 10 minutes is sufficient. Liver should be pink on the inside. Sprinkle bacon bits over the liver before serving. Serves 4.

Cabbage Stuffed Pierogi
Pierożki z Kapusty

FILLING:

1 pound boiled cabbage
½ pound dry cottage cheese
1 minced onion
2 tablespoons butter
salt and pepper to taste

DOUGH:

2 eggs
3¼ cups flour
dash salt
¼ cup water
3 tablespoons butter
3 tablespoons bread crumbs

Drain cabbage and chop coarsely. (A blender works well here.) Combine with the cottage cheese. Lightly sauté the onion in the butter. Combine with cabbage-cheese mixture and season to taste.

To make dough, combine the eggs, flour and salt. If necessary, add a little water to get desired consistency to knead a smooth, loose dough. Roll out very thinly and cut into 3-inch squares. Place a teaspoon of the filling on each square. Fold over to form a triangle and pinch the edges together.

Cook several at a time in a large pot of boiling, salted water for 5 minutes, or until they rise to the top. Remove with a slotted spoon and keep warm until all are finished.

Drizzle the buttered bread crumbs over the pierogi just before serving.

Carrots are often maligned through no fault of their own. Supermarkets usually only supply carrots with the size and tenderness of bludgeons. If you can, find young carrots, harvested while still slim and only about 4 inches long for a mouthwatering treat, the basis of this next recipe.

Baby Carrots Polonaise
Młoda Marchewka po Polsku

2 bunches baby carrots
1 teaspoon sugar
dash salt

Scour the carrots with a vegetable brush. (Do not peel.) Place in 1½ cups boiling water to which the sugar and salt has been added. Simmer, tightly covered, for 10 to 12 minutes. Drain, and garnish with buttered bread crumbs.

Buttered Bread Crumbs

Use equal amounts of butter and dry bread crumbs. Melt the butter over low heat, then add the crumbs. Sauté for 5 minutes or until lightly toasted, while stirring constantly to prevent burning.

Cracklings, also known as kindling, are a crispy, cookie-like pastry that resembles sticks, or kindling wood; hence its name. Following are three versions of the same recipe.

Cracklings
Chrusty

I

¼ *cup butter*
1 *cup flour*
3 *egg yolks*
1 *egg*
¼ *cup sugar*
½ *teaspoon bicarbonate of soda*
½ *cup light cream*
salt to taste
honey

Combine the butter and the flour; add remaining ingredients to form a smooth paste. Roll out thin and cut into 4 × 1-inch strips.

Make a short, lengthwise slit in the center of each strip, and pass the other end of the strip through the slit. Repeat until all the dough has been used. Deep-fry until golden brown. Drain and serve with honey.

II

2 *cups flour, sifted*
2 *tablespoons butter*
2 *tablespoons sugar*
2 *eggs*
1 *tablespoon vinegar*
½ *cup sour cream*

Combine the flour, butter, sugar and eggs. Gradually stir in the vinegar and sour cream and knead until solid enough to roll. (Extra flour may be necessary.) Proceed as in I.

Note: A piece of raw potato placed in the hot oil will eliminate much of the odor of frying. A piece of bread added to the hot fat will keep the oil from spitting, or splashing out.

III

8 egg yolks
8 tablespoons sugar
1⅓ cups light cream
3 tablespoons rum
2½ cups flour

Beat the egg yolks with the sugar. Add the cream and rum. Gradually mix the flour into the batter until it is solid enough to roll out. Proceed with the rest of the directions as in I.

SPRING LUNCH FOR 4

Sour Cream Cucumbers and Onion Rings Arranged on
Crisp Spinach Leaves /
Ogórki z Cebulą w Smietanie na Liściach Szpinakowych
Endive with Fresh Mayonnaise / Endywia z Majonezem
Hard-cooked Egg Flowerettes / Różyczki z Jajek
Coddled Fish Fillets in Shrimp Sauce /
Ryba Duszona w Sosie Rakowym
Potato Pancakes I / Placki Kartoflane
Fruit Cream with Wine / Przetarte Owoce z Winem

Polish food has been influenced by many countries. Geographically, Poland has been situated at the crossroads of East and West. Poland has seen many regimes and many alliances with foreign royalty: French, Czech, Saxon, Hungarian and Italian.

41

The Sforza princess, who became Queen Bona, introduced green vegetables and tomatoes to Poland. Her own cooks and chefs taught the native royal staff to cook the greens, and eventually the novel fare found its way to the peasants' cottages and gardens. Even today the Polish word for green vegetables is wloszcyzna, which means, "things Italian".

Sour Cream Cucumbers and Onion Rings Arranged on Crisp Spinach Leaves

Ogórki z Cebulą w Smietanie na Liściach Szpinakowych

1 cucumber, peeled
1 medium-sized onion, peeled
½ cup sour cream
salt to taste
4 hard-cooked eggs
spinach leaves, rinsed and drained
½ cup olive oil
juice of ½ lemon
fresh ground pepper

Slice the cucumbers and onion as finely as possible. Toss with the sour cream and salt and set aside. Shell the eggs, and slice the eggs into halves with ridges to resemble flowerettes. Arrange the spinach leaves on a chilled platter. Mound the cucumber and onion salad in the center of the leaves and flank with the flowerettes (see next page). Combine the olive oil and lemon juice, and pour over all. Grind fresh pepper over the top for an added fillip.

Endive with Fresh Mayonnaise

Endywia z Majonezem

6 heads endive
½ cup freshly made mayonnaise
salt to taste
2 tablespoons honey
2 tablespoons celery vinegar, OR
other vinegar
lettuce leaves
6 cherry tomatoes
egg flowerettes (see below)

Rinse endive, and slice diagonally into 1-inch segments. Prepare the mayonnaise. Combine and toss the endive, salt, mayonnaise, honey and vinegar. Arrange the endive mixture on a crisp bed of lettuce leaves. Garnish with the cherry tomatoes and egg flowerettes.

Hard-cooked Egg Flowerettes

Różyczki z Jajek

For the above recipe, use 6 hard-cooked eggs. Make the flowerettes by shelling the chilled eggs, then slicing each egg in half in a zigzag pattern.

Celery Vinegar II

2 *cups white vinegar*
1 *teaspoon salt, or to taste*
2 *cups minced celery roots*
¼ *teaspoon celery seeds*
6 *peppercorns*

Combine all ingredients but the celery roots and bring to a boil. Add the celery roots and boil for another 5 minutes. Pour into a sterilized wide-mouthed bottle and seal. Allow the flavors to marry for 2 to 3 weeks. Strain through cheesecloth into a sterilized pint bottle.

The earliest mention of Polish cuisine is found in the writings of Roman historian Tacitus, who lived during the first century A.D. He described Polish food as being "of a simple kind". Hunters, fishermen, and primitive agrarians, they lived on breads made of barley, oats and millet; gruels, milk, cheese, wild berries and fruits, and on wild game, fowl and fish.

When Christianity conquered Europe, its influence developed beyond religion, and into art, mores, daily life styles and even diet. Aside from administering to religious needs, Christian monks also kept orchards, vineyards and gardens and generally brought a higher standard of food production to the peoples of their communities.

Charlemagne united most of the European nations into a single kingdom around 800 A.D. Among other political attributes, he also gave his people advice on dietary plans and on how to plant herb gardens and vineyards. Gradually, cultivated grains and domestic animals became more common and replaced much of the wild game and fowl eaten at the Polish tables. However, one favorite food continued to be popular from the Middle Ages to today: fish. People of the Dark Ages ate considerable amounts of trout, pike and carp, which then, as now, were readily available. Recipes for fish abound.

The Polish also make wide use of crayfish, but most of the recipes calling for crayfish are flexible enough to allow for the substitution of shrimp.

Coddled Fish Fillets in Shrimp Sauce

Ryba Duszona w Sosie Rakowym

½ cup butter
7 cups light cream (or half-and-half)
salt and pepper to taste
½ pound fresh mushrooms, chopped
parsley (optional)
½ cup sifted flour
1 teaspoon paprika
2 pounds fish fillets
1 pound med. shrimp, parboiled OR
    1 pound crayfish, parboiled

Make a roux of the melted butter and flour in the top of a double boiler. Add cream slowly, stirring continuously. Mix in the spices, and simmer for 5 minutes. Do not boil.

Slice fish fillets down center. Begin at the widest end of the fillet and roll up. Secure each fillet with a toothpick. Place rolled-up fillets in sauce and simmer for about 10 minutes, covered. Shell and devein the shrimp (or crayfish). Add the mushrooms and shrimp to the sauce and heat through. Remove toothpicks, arrange fish and sauce on a warmed platter, and garnish with parsley and serve immediately.

Potato Pancakes
Placki Kartoflane

I

6 potatoes
1 cup milk
4 tablespoons butter
3 eggs, separated
dash nutmeg
salt to taste

Boil potatoes and mash. Combine with milk and egg yolks. Sprinkle in nutmeg. Whip egg whites until stiff and fold into potato mixture. Sauté in butter until golden brown.

II

½ cup bacon drippings
8 large grated potatoes
2 eggs
salt to taste
1 large minced onion
4 tablespoons flour

Heat the bacon drippings until sizzling. Combine the other ingredients well; mixture will be thick. Roll into balls in the palm of your hand. Flatten each ball into a "cake" with a fork. Sauté in the bacon drippings until golden.

Fruit cream is a traditional fruit dessert that is similar to a pudding or fruit pie filling in consistency. It can be made with almost any kind of berry; strawberries, gooseberries, currants, cranberries, and even cut-up fruit, such as apples, can be substituted.

Fruit Cream with Wine

Przetarte Owoce z Winem

6 cups berries
5 cups water
2 cups sugar OR *honey*
1 cinnamon stick
4 whole cloves
3 tablespoons cornstarch OR *potato flour*
2 tablespoons grated lemon rind
1 cup white wine

Whirl berries with the water in a blender (or mash) to purée. (It is desirable at this point to strain the juice to remove seeds.) Combine with the sugar, cinnamon and cloves and simmer for 15 minutes. Remove the spices. Mix the flour or starch with the wine until smooth, then add to the berry mixture along with the lemon rind. Stir continuously over medium heat until thickened; about 5 to 7 minutes. Moisten your prettiest mold, sprinkle the inside with sugar and fill with the berry pudding. Chill several hours, or overnight.

Note: When cooking with whole spices it is easier to remove them if they've first been placed in a cheesecloth packet.

SPRING CELEBRATION FOR 4

Succulent Rhubarb and Carrot Relish /
Soczysta Sałatka z Rabarbaru i Marchewki
Eggs à la Polonaise / Jajka a la Polonaise
Toasted Bread Triangles / Przypiekane Połówki Chleba
Braised Spring Lamb with Cabbage / Jagnię w Kapuście
Baked Potato with Mushroom Topping /
Kartofle Wypiekane z Grzybami
Fruit Bombe / Bomba Owocowa

The most delicate of Springs' flavors and colors are combined in this menu. The muted seasonings enhance the natural savoriness of the vegetables and the meat. The pink of the lamb and rhubarb combined with the brighter hues of the fruits and berries make these dishes a tempting sight on a balmy spring day.

Succulent Rhubarb and Carrot Relish
Soczysta Sałatka z Rabarbaru i Marchewki

3 stalks rhubarb, sliced diagonally into ½-inch pieces
4 carrots, peeled and grated
2 tablespoons sugar or to taste
salt to taste
4 tablespoons sour cream
lettuce leaves
chopped parsley

Combine the first five ingredients, then arrange on lettuce. Garnish with chopped parsley, and serve on a chilled platter.

Eggs à la Polonaise
Jajka a la Polonaise

2 eggs per person
one pat sweet butter per egg
salt to taste

Soft-cook the eggs—3 to 4 minutes. Remove the eggs from the shells and spoon into individual, elegant glasses. Add butter, salt as you wish, and serve immediately.

Toasted Bread Triangles
Przypiekane Połówki Chleba

Trim 8 slices of bread of all crust and slice diagonally to form triangles. Butter lightly, and toast under the broiler for a few moments.

Braised Spring Lamb with Cabbage
Jagnię w Kapuście

2 pounds lamb, cut into serving pieces
4 tablespoons flour
4 tablespoons butter
2 cups chicken stock, OR
   water
3 cloves garlic, sliced
salt to taste
1 head cabbage, quartered
1½ teaspoons caraway seeds
1 teaspoon sugar, or honey
2 teaspoons vinegar

Dredge the lamb in flour and brown on all sides in the butter. Add the stock or water and simmer for 1 to 1½ hours. Add all the remaining ingredients and continue cooking over medium heat for another 30 minutes, stirring occasionally. Serves 4.

Note: When purchasing lamb, look for light pink, lean meat. The color darkens with age.

Baked Potato with Mushroom Topping

Kartofle Wypiekane z Grzybami

4 large baking potatoes
½ pound fresh mushrooms, chopped
1 finely chopped onion
½ cup butter
1 egg
2 teaspoons parsley
2 tablespoons light cream, OR
    half-and-half
1 cup sour cream
4 tablespoons grated cheese
½ cup buttered bread crumbs

Bake potatoes at 375°F for 45 minutes, or until potatoes are tender when pierced through with a fork. Slice lengthwise, scoop out and mash the pulp. Lightly sauté the mushrooms and onion in butter, then combine with the mashed potato centers, the egg, parsley and cream. Blend well, then return to the potato shells. Generously top with the sour cream and garnish with the grated cheese and bread crumbs. Return to the oven at 325°F for a few minutes to warm through.
Note: This recipe can be used as a light meal all by itself.

Fruit Bomb

Bomba Owocowa

3 cups fruit or berries
3 cups whipping cream
3 cups sugar
fresh fruit or berries for garnish

Whirl chopped fruit or berries in blender, or mash until puréed. Whip cream, adding sugar gradually, until stiff. Slowly add fruit purée to the cream, while continuously beating. When thoroughly blended, set in freezer. After 1½ hours remove from freezer and beat again to prevent icing and to improve the texture. Return to freezer. Repeat this procedure again after an hour, then transfer to a sugared mold and leave in freezer for at least 2 more hours. Garnish with fresh fruit or berries.

SPRING PARTY FOR 4

Peas and Ripe Tomato Salad /
Sałatka z Groszku i Świeżych Pomidorów
Eggs with Cream in Ramekins /
Jaja na Śmietanie w Miseczce
Veal Simmered with Apples / Cielęcina Duszona z Jabłkami
Buckwheat Groats / Kasza Gryczana
Braised Carrots / Marchewka Duszona
Strawberry Tarts / Truskawki w Muszelkach z Ciasta

Veal is another delectable Spring dish. Combined with Eggs with Cream in Ramekins, it makes an unbeatable base for an April party.

Peas and Ripe Tomato Salad
Sałatka z Groszku i Świeżych Pomidorów

3 tomatoes, quartered
lettuce leaves
2 cups peas, cooked and drained
½ cup sour cream
2 tablespoons chopped parsley

Arrange tomato wedges on lettuce leaves. Spoon chilled peas over tomatoes. Dress with the sour cream and garnish with the parsley. Serve on chilled plates. Serves 4.

Eggs with Cream in Ramekins
Jaja na Śmietanie w Miseczce

butter for preparing ramekins
8|eggs
1½ cups light cream, OR
  half-and-half
½ cup grated cheese
salt and pepper to taste

Butter 4 ramekins or other individual baking dishes. Scald the cream and pour into the ramekins. Gently break in the eggs, being careful not to break the yolks. Add salt or pepper, if desired. Place the dishes in a pan of hot water and bake at 350°F until the eggs begin to set (about 10 minutes). Then sprinkle with grated cheese and return to oven to finish cooking. Serves 4.

Veal Simmered with Apples

Cielecina Duszona z Jab*l*kami

2 pounds thinly sliced veal
3 tablespoons flour
3 tablespoons butter
2 cups beef stock
2 apples, peeled, pared and sliced

Dredge the veal in the flour and lightly sauté in butter. Remove meat. Gradually add the beef stock to the roux in the pan, stirring constantly to prevent lumping. Then add the apple slices to the liquid. Simmer for 10 minutes. Return the veal to the mixture and simmer another 5 minutes. Serves 4.

The best time to buy veal is late winter or spring. The meat should be very pale, almost white, with only a faint pink coloration. Veal has no exterior fat or marbling.

A rule of thumb to remember when buying veal is:
Buy ¾–1 pound bone-in meat per serving
Buy ⅓–½ pound boneless meat per serving

Buckwheat Groats

Kasza Gryczana

1 cup buckwheat groats
2 tablespoons butter
1 egg (optional)
2 cups boiling salted water

Coat the groats with the melted butter, and, if you wish, with the lightly beaten egg. Mix well and allow to dry. After about 10 minutes, stir groats into boiling water and simmer for 10 more minutes. Cover and bake at 350°F for 45 minutes. Serves 4. (A Dutch oven works well here.)

Braised Carrots
Marchewka Duszona

8 young carrots, peeled and sliced diagonally
3 tablespoons butter
½ cup court bouillon OR
*   salted water*
1 teaspoon dill

Sauté carrot slices in butter lightly. Add the bouillon, cover and steam for 15 to 20 minutes. Garnish with fresh dill. Serves 4 generously.

Strawberry Tarts
Truskawki w Muszelkach z Ciasta

PASTRY:

1 cup sweet butter
2 cups flour, sifted
¾ cup sugar
5 egg yolks
1 ounce yeast

4 cups cleaned and hulled strawberries

MERINGUE:

5 egg whites
1¼ cups sugar

Cut butter into flour with a pastry blender. Mix in sugar and egg yolks, then add the yeast. Knead dough lightly and roll onto greased cookie sheet. Bake at 350°F for 10 to 15 minutes.

Arrange strawberries on top of cake.

Whip egg whites, adding sugar gradually, until very stiff. Cover the berries with the meringue and bake at 325°F for 25 to 30 minutes. While still warm from the oven, slice into squares.

EASTER DINNER FOR 10

Hard-Cooked Easter Eggs / Jajka Wielkanocne na Twardo
Potato Salad / Sałata z Ziemniaków
Beets and Horseradish Relish / Ćwikła z Chrzanem
Horseradish Sauce / Sos Chrzanowy
Boiled Crayfish / Raki Gotowane
Polish Sausage / Kiełbasa Polska
Baked Ham / Szynka Pieczona
Roast Turkey / Pieczony Indyk
Shrimp (or Crayfish) Stuffing / Nadzienie z Raczków
Raisin Stuffing / Nadzienie z Rodzynkami
Chestnut Stuffing / Nadzienie z Maronów
Easter Baba / Babka Wielkanocna
Date Mazurek / Mazurek Daktylowy
Orange Mazurek / Mazurek Pomarańczowy
Raisin Mazurek / Mazurek z Rodzynkami
Gypsy Mazur / Mazurek Cygański

Most Poles are Roman Catholics, and Lent is observed most strictly. So when Easter arrives, it is celebrated with gusto. All the forbidden meats of the past forty days are to be sampled along with a variety of other delicacies. Easter dinner, which occurs at midday, is a festive occasion and gourmets' delight.

The many dishes are prepared on Good Friday and Holy Saturday. Everything is chilled, except for a barshch which can be quickly reheated on Easter Sunday after church.

Easter eggs are generally blessed by the priest in Polish communities. When brought home again, they are shelled and quartered before they are served at the Easter dinner table.

The kielbasa may be boiled, chilled, then sliced and served as an accompaniment to the other dishes.

Potato Salad
Sałata z Ziemniaków

8 potatoes
1 finely chopped onion
½ to ⅔ cup olive oil
¼ cup vinegar
2 tablespoons olive oil (optional)

Pare, peel and cook potatoes in salt water. Drain and while still hot combine with the onion, olive oil and vinegar. Toss gently, or you'll end up with mashed potatoes. The warm potatoes tend to absorb more oil than chilled potatoes. You may require another tablespoon or two of oil after the salad has cooled.

Beet and Horseradish Relish
Ćwikła z Chrzanem

2 pounds cooked beets
2 tablespoons horseradish sauce
1 teaspoon sugar

Whirl ingredients in blender until coarsely chopped. Cover and let stand in refrigerator for 2 days to blend.

Horseradish Sauce

Sos Chrzanowy

2 tablespoons horseradish, freshly grated
⅔ cup sour cream
1 teaspoon sugar
1 teaspoon vinegar
dash salt

Mix all ingredients and allow to stand several hours, tightly covered, in the refrigerator to blend thoroughly.

Boiled Crayfish

Raki Gotowane

10 live crayfish
salt to taste
2 quarts boiling water
fresh dill

Wash the live crayfish and cook the same way as you would live lobster, that is by throwing them headfirst (to avoid any suffering) into rapidly boiling salted water. Add fresh dill and boil for 15 minutes. Serve hot with drawn butter.

Baked Ham
Szynka Pieczona

MARINADE:

2 cups water
1 cup vinegar
1 sliced onion
3 bay leaves
6 whole cloves
1 stick cinnamon

Combine all ingredients; boil for 10 minutes.

5 pounds uncooked ham
3 tablespoons bacon drippings

Marinate the raw ham in the vinegar mixture overnight. Turn ham occasionally.

Bake ham at 450°F for 20 minutes and baste with the bacon drippings. Reduce oven temperature to 300°F and baste every 20 minutes for another 2 hours (25 to 30 minutes per pound).

Roast Turkey
Pieczony Indyk

1 turkey (10 to 12 pounds)
salt to taste
turkey liver and gizzards (optional)
1 stick butter OR
    ½ cup bacon drippings

Carefully rinse and dry the turkey inside and out. Rub skin with butter or bacon drippings. Lightly fill with one of the following stuffings and sew or skewer closed. Tie legs together and tuck wings behind back.

Place bird breast-side-up on a rack in roasting pan and roast for 4½ to 5 hours at 325°F (about 25 minutes per pound of weight before stuffing). Test for doneness by pricking the inside of the thigh with a fork. If pink juice trickles out, the meat is not yet done.

Shrimp (or Crayfish) Stuffing
Nadzienie z Raczków

20 baby shrimp OR
*   10 crayfish, cooked, shelled and chopped finely*
½ pound mushrooms
½ cup butter
turkey liver, sautéed and mashed
3 eggs
1 cup bread crumbs
broth to moisten

Clean the shrimp. Sauté the shrimp or crayfish and mushrooms in the butter. Combine all remaining ingredients, and stuff the turkey.

Raisin Stuffing I
Nadzienie z Rodzykami

turkey liver
2 tablespoons butter
2 eggs, separated
⅔ cup bread crumbs
grated nutmeg
salt to taste
3 whole cloves
2 tablespoons parsley
½ cup golden raisins
cream to moisten

Sauté and mash the liver in the butter, then combine with the egg yolks. Mix in everything but the egg whites. Beat egg whites stiff and fold into the mixture. Loosely stuff the turkey and roast. Allow an extra half hour or so roasting time for the stuffing (which rises a little and should be well done).

Chestnut Stuffing
Nadzienie z Maronów

2½ cups chopped chestnuts
½ cup celery
½ cup butter
2 eggs
4 cups bread cubes
½ chopped onion
salt and pepper to taste

Slice a cross in each chestnut, then boil in salted water for 15 to 20 minutes. Remove shell and dark membrane, then chop the chestnuts finely. Sauté the celery in butter. Combine all ingredients, stuff the bird, and allow about an extra ½ hour roasting time for the stuffing.

Easter Baba
Babka Wielkanocna

1 envelope dry yeast
½ cup light cream OR
half-and-half
⅓ cup sugar
2 cups flour
3 eggs
1 teaspoon vanilla
½ teaspoon almond extract
1 teaspoon grated lemon
1 tablespoon melted butter
¼ cup raisins

Dissolve yeast in cream. Combine with half the sugar and flour and let double in size. Add all the remaining ingredients except the raisins and knead until smooth. Add the raisins, while continuing to knead. Grease and dust baba pan with flour. Place dough in pan, cover with a clean cloth, and leave in a very warm, draft-free place until doubled in size. Bake at 350°F for 35 to 40 minutes. When cool, remove from pan and drizzle with icing.

Baba Icing
Lukrowa Babka

½ cup confectioners sugar
1 tablespoon rum OR
lemon juice

Mix well and lightly drizzle over the baba. Easter isn't Easter without a selection of mazureks, which are a sort of chewy cakelike cookie square. Choose one or several of the following recipes.

Date Mazurek I

Mazurek Daktylowy

DOUGH:

1 cup butter
3 cups flour
1 cup confectioners sugar
2½ teaspoons baking powder
3 eggs
4 tablespoons sour cream

Cut butter into flour. Combine with the sugar and baking powder. Add the eggs, one at a time, and the sour cream and knead dough for 10 minutes, or until smooth. Chill for 1 hour, or until firm, then roll thin and place on greased or stickproof baking sheet. Spread dough to cover entire pan. Bake at 375°F for 10 to 15 minutes.

TOPPING:

1 whole lemon
1 cup·sugar
⅓ cup water
1 cup pitted chopped dates
1 cup chopped walnuts
½ cup candied orange peel (see recipe below.)

Chop lemon and whirl in blender until puréed, or grate the rind and pulp, taking care to remove the seeds. Combine all ingredients and cook over medium heat for 10 to 15 minutes, or until thickened. Spread the topping evenly over the cake. Frost with the following icing when cake has cooled.

ICING:

2 *cups confectioners sugar*
3 *tablespoons lemon juice*

Combine and mix until smooth. Frost and slice into squares.

Candied Orange Peel

2 *cups orange peel, sliced into thin strips*
boiling water
1⅔ *cups sugar*
⅓ *cup water*

Simmer the orange strips in boiling water for 2 hours. (After the first hour change the water to prevent a bitter taste.) Drain the peel and allow to dry. Combine the peels, sugar and ⅓ cup water and simmer for 15 minutes, or until thickened. Drain and dry the peels overnight. Save the syrup and reheat the next day until it forms a thread (about 230° to 234°F). Coat each peel separately and dry in a slow oven.

Date Mazurek II

Mazurek Daktylowy II

7 *egg whites*
2 *cups sugar*
2¼ *cups ground or very finely chopped almonds*
2 *cups pitted chopped dates*
½ *pound grated, bittersweet chocolate*

Beat egg whites until stiff while slowly adding sugar. Add the rest of the ingredients and blend well. Grease and flour a cookie sheet and spread mixture over it evenly. Bake at 200°F for 25 minutes. Cool and frost with the following icing.

ICING:
1 cup sugar
¼ cup water
1 tablespoon lemon juice

Cook sugar and water until syrup spins a thread (about 230° to 234°F). Then whirl in blender or beat with a wooden spoon until mixture thickens. Cool, then blend in the lemon juice. Frost cake and let set before slicing into squares.

Orange Mazurek
Mazurek Pomarańczowy

2 cups ground almonds
1 cup sugar
juice of 1 lemon

Grease and dust a cookie sheet with flour. Mix the ingredients to form a paste that will spread. Place mixture evenly on pan and bake at 200°F for 15 minutes.

TOPPING:
1 lemon
2 oranges
2 cups sugar
½ cup orange juice

Grate both the pulp and the rinds of the lemon and oranges, removing only the seeds, or chop coarsely, and purée in blender. Combine all ingredients and cook over medium heat until mixture thickens. Cool, then beat lightly with a wooden spoon until mixture begins to take on a pearlized, or frosted, coloration. Then spread on the cake and let set before slicing.

Raisin Mazurek

Mazurek z Rodzynkami

2 cups golden raisins
2 cups finely chopped almonds
2 eggs
1 cup sugar
3 tablespoons grated lemon rind

Mix all ingredients thoroughly. Grease and flour a cookie sheet. Pour mixture evenly over tin and bake for 25 minutes at 200°F. Top with the same topping used for the Orange Mazurek.

Gypsy Mazur

Mazurek Cygański

6 egg whites
½ cup sugar
6 egg yolks, lightly beaten
1 teaspoon vanilla extract
1 cup chopped figs
1 cup pitted chopped dates
1 cup raisins
½ cup candied orange rind
1¾ cups crushed walnuts
3 tablespoons grated lemon rind
6 tablespoons cornstarch

Whip egg whites, gradually adding sugar until meringue forms peaks. Beat in the yolks and vanilla, then combine with the fruit mixture, which has been blended with the cornstarch. Place on greased and floured cookie sheet and bake at 325°F for 30 minutes.

Summer Menus

Summer approaches with a ripening of produce and spirit. Now there is a wide choice of fruits and vegetables available both in the garden and in the market. Yet because of Summer's heady warmth, chilled meals are ardently welcomed. Following are a few frosty feasts.

SUMMER CELEBRATION FOR 4

Summer Salad / Sałatka Letnia
Baked Omelet with Wine Sauce /
Omlety Wypiekane w Sosie w Winnym
Cream of Cauliflower Soup with Buttered Croutons /
Zupa Kalafiorowa z Grzankami
Lamb Birds / Baranie Ptaszki
Fresh Seasonal Fruit Tray / Taca Świeżych Owoców

Here is an elegant commencement for a special Sunday.
The opulence of the meal can be set off by your own
combination of jewels of fresh fruits.

Summer Salad

Sałatka Letnia

1 head lettuce
1 cucumber, peeled and sliced
1 bunch radishes, sliced
2 carrots, peeled and sliced diagonally
½ cup sour cream
salt to taste
½ teaspoon sugar
snipped chives

Wash lettuce and break into bite-sized pieces. Toss with the cucumber, carrot and radish slices. Prepare the sour cream and seasonings for the dressing. Spoon over salad and garnish with the snipped chives.

Baked Omelet with Wine Sauce

Omlety Wypiekane w Sosie w Winnym

6 egg yolks
6 egg whites, stiffly beaten
6 tablespoons flour
salt to taste
Wine Sauce

Beat egg yolks in the top of a double boiler over barely simmering water until creamy. Cool, then combine with the whipped egg whites. Slowly add the flour and salt. Spoon into a torte pan and bake at 375°F for 20 minutes, or until set. Serve with wine sauce.

Wine Sauce / Sos z Wina

4 eggs yolks
2 tablespoons honey
2 cups white wine
grated lemon peel (optional)

Beat the egg yolks in the top of a double boiler over barely simmering water with the honey. Add the wine and continue cooking until sauce thickens. If desired, add grated lemon peel. Spoon over the baked omelet while piping hot.

Cream of Cauliflower Soup with Buttered Croutons

Zupa Kalafiorowa z Grzankami

1 quart chicken stock
2 cups cauliflower flowerets
½ cup heavy cream
2 tablespoons flour
1 egg yolk
1 teaspoon fresh dill

Simmer cauliflower in the chicken stock for 20 to 30 minutes. Combine the cream, flour and egg yolk with a whisk. Add 1 cup chicken stock to the cream mixture, then gradually pour the cream mixture into the remaining stock, stirring constantly. Simmer for 10 to 15 minutes. Do not boil. Garnish with the dill.

Buttered Croutons / Grzanki

2 tablespoons melted butter
2 slices stale bread, cubed

Combine and toss until evenly coated. Bake at 350°F for about 20 minutes, or until lightly browned.

Lamb Birds

Baranie Ptaszki

1½ pounds boneless lamb
¼ cup flour, sifted
salt to taste
2 tablespoons butter
8 shallots, sliced
½ cup sliced mushrooms
1 tablespoon tomato paste
¼ cup chianti or other dry red wine

Slice lamb thinly, as for scalloppine. Pound the lamb slices, then dip in seasoned flour. Brown quickly in the butter. Place the meat in a baking dish, top with the vegetables. Combine the tomato paste with the wine and pour over all. Bake at 325°F for 40 minutes.

SUMMER LUNCHEON FOR 4

Frosty Artichoke Salad /
Sałatka z Zielonych Artyczoków z Majonezem
Flybanes / Muchomory
Marinated Veal / Cielęcina Marynowana
Potato Round Bread / Okrągły Chleb Kartoflany
Chilled Blueberry Soup / Chłodnik Borówkowy

There's nothing more refreshing in July than a chilled *déjeuner*. These frosty delectables will cajole even the most jaded of appetites. Be sure to try the Flybanes, an ingenious piece of epicurean camouflage that uses hardcooked eggs for the stems and tomato halves for the tops of "mushrooms."

Frosty Artichoke Salad
Sałatka z Zielonych Artyczoków z Majonezem

> 4 fresh artichokes
> boiling water to cover artichokes
> juice of 1 lemon
> 2 teaspoons sugar
> salt to taste

Remove the coarse bottom leaves and trim the stems of the artichokes. Immerse the green artichokes in boiling water. Add the remaining ingredients and cook for 40 to 45 minutes. Remove the artichokes, stand upside down to drain, then chill thoroughly. Garnish with mayonnaise.

Flybanes
Muchomory

> 4 hard-cooked eggs
> 2 tomatoes, halved lengthwise
> salt to taste
> mayonnaise
> fresh greens

Chill and shell the eggs. Slice a little off each end. Stand the eggs upright to resemble mushroom stems. Place a tomato half over each egg as a mushroom cap. Serve on a bed of lettuce greens and garnish with mayonnaise.

Marinated Veal

Cielęcina Marynowana

2 pounds veal rump, boned
2 cups milk

Soak veal in milk overnight. Remove meat, wipe with a
damp cloth (give the milk to your pet—he'll love you for
it), and cover with the marinade.

MARINADE:

1½ cups water
½ cup cider vinegar
2 whole cloves
6 peppercorns
1 bay leaf

Combine these five ingredients. Boil for 5 minutes. Pour
over the veal to cover entirely. Refrigerate for 3 days to
allow flavors to blend. Then add 2 sliced carrots, 2 sliced
onions, and 1 sliced leek to the marinade, roll up the
veal, tie with a string, and simmer for 1½ hours over
medium heat, stirring occasionally. Remove the meat
from the marinade, chill thoroughly, and serve cut into
very thin slices.

Potato Round Bread

Okrągły Chleb Kartoflany

½ cup milk
½ cup mashed potatoes
3 tablespoons sugar
2 tablespoons butter
3 cups flour
1 egg, beaten
1 package active dry yeast
4 tablespoons warm water
salt to taste
1 tablespoon flour, about

Scald the milk, then add the potatoes, sugar and butter. When cooled, add half the flour and the egg. Dissolve the yeast in the water and combine with the potato mixture and salt. Cover with a cloth and set in a warm place for about 1½ hours. Add the rest of the flour, or enough to form a stiff dough. Knead for about 10 minutes and set in a greased bowl. Cover; allow to rise until doubled. Punch down. Shape into a round loaf. Cover and let rise until doubled again. Slice an X on top of the bread and sift a few grains of flour over the loaf. Bake at 350°F for about 45 minutes.

Chilled Blueberry Soup
Chłodnik Borówkowy

1 pint fresh blueberries
2 cups water
2 teaspoons cooked rice OR
    uncooked fast-cooking rice
¼ teaspoon cinnamon
dash of ground cloves
¼ cup sugar
½ cup sour cream for garnish

Combine all ingredients except the sour cream and simmer over medium heat for about 10 minutes. Swirl mixture in blender until smooth, then chill. Serve in frosted sherbet glasses, garnished with sour cream.

SUMMER DINNER FOR 4

Tangy Apple and Leek Salad /
Pikantna Sałatka z Jabłek i Porów
Summer Compote / Kompot Letni
Roasted Guinea Hen / Pieczona Panterka
Crepes à la Polonaise / Polskie Naleśniki

This summer menu is truly an inventive medley of flavors. Enjoy the season's bounty with each of these recipes. Particularly notable is the Summer Compote which can be prepared as directed by the recipe, or which can be left to your imagination as to the fruits used.

Tangy Apple and Leek Salad
Pikantna Sałatka z Jabłek i Porów

2 apples, peeled, cored and chopped
2 leeks, finely chopped
1 tablespoon lemon juice
½ cup mayonnaise
watercress
romaine

Combine the first four ingredients and arrange on the greens.

Summer Compote
Kompot Letni

1 cup sauturne or other sweet white wine
1 cup orange juice

Combine wine and orange juice and pour over your own assortment of freshly sliced fruits and berries, or use the following suggestions as a guide:

1 cup raspberries
1 cup sliced strawberries
1 cup melon balls

Toss VERY gently.

Roasted Guinea Hen
Pieczona Panterka

¼ *cup olive oil*
2 *tablespoons lemon juice*
2 *guinea hens*
1 *tablespoon salt, or, to taste*
½ *cup butter*

Combine the oil and lemon juice. Thoroughly rub into the skins of the two birds. Cover and refrigerate overnight, or for up to 48 hours, for the flavors to marry. Wipe the excess oil and lemon off before baking hens. Salt and roast in a 350°F oven for 1¼ hours or until tender. Baste with butter as necessary. Serves 4.

Crêpes à la Polonaise
Polskie Naleśniki

4 *crêpes, prepared, (see Index)*
1 *cup small-curd cottage cheese, sieved*
1 *egg*
1 *teaspoon finely chopped candied orange rind, see Index*
¼ *cup finely chopped almonds*
¼ *cup raisins*
2 *tablespoons sugar*
2 *tablespoons butter*
sour cream

Warm the prepared crêpes. Combine all other ingredients except butter and sour cream and divide mixture onto centers of the crêpes. Roll up crêpes, completely enclosing filling. Melt the butter in a skillet, and lightly brown the crêpes in the butter. Serve on heated platter and garnish with sour cream.

SUMMER BRUNCH FOR 12 (OR MORE)

Pickled Mushrooms / Grzyby Marynowane
Individual Oyster Soufflés / Dołki z Ostrygami
Roast Suckling Pig / Pieczony Prosiak
Raisin Stuffing / Nadzienie z Rodzynkami
Fresh Peas with Dill Butter /
Groszek z Masłem Koperkowym
Peach Tarts and Plum Tarts /
Brzoskwinie i Śliwki w Muszelkach z Ciasta

What is more enjoyable than a warm summer's day with the sunlight filtering through trees laden with ripening fruit? Now is a time to savor the luscious results of a fertile terrain. Laze in the sun after a feast of Roast Suckling Pig and Oyster Soufflé. Life is good; have the crowd over for brunch! Celebrate a wedding or a holiday or even just the good weather with a special group of friends. All the recipes for the following brunch have been expanded to serve a dozen (or more) people. The Individual Oyster Soufflés (which are deceivingly simple to prepare) add a sumptuous touch.

Pickled Mushrooms

Grzyby Marynowane

Cook these delicatessen dainties ahead of time for a better melding of flavors, and to allow yourself more time for the preparation of last minute recipes.

> *2 pounds fresh mushrooms*
> *2 finely chopped onions*
> *1 cup water, salted*
> *½ cup vinegar, or to taste*
> *4 bay leaves*
> *¼ cup peppercorns*
> *1 tablespoon allspice*

Combine all the ingredients, bring to a boil, then simmer for about 15 minutes. When cooled, remove the mushrooms to glass containers for storage in the refrigerator until needed. If storing for any extended length of time, be sure to use sterilized jars and caps.

Individual Oyster Soufflés

Dołki z Ostrygami

> *1 quart oysters*
> *¼ cup flour*
> *¼ cup butter*
> *2 cups half-and-half*
> *salt to taste*
> *6 egg yolks, beaten*
> *6 egg whites*

Chop oysters coarsely and drain. Make a roux of the flour and butter. Gradually add the half-and-half, stirring constantly. Stir in all the ingredients except the egg whites. Remove from heat. Whip the egg whites until stiff, then fold into the other ingredients. Spoon mixture into 12 greased, individual ramekins. Bake at 350°F for 20 minutes, or until lightly browned.

Roast Suckling Pig

Pieczony Prosiak

1 10-lb. whole suckling pig
½ cup butter
salt to taste
1 cup beer

Wash the pig well and pat dry. Rub butter between your hands, then rub the meat with your buttered hands. Work the butter in, then salt. Stuff the suckling pig with the following stuffing, then sew shut or secure with small skewers. Place in a large shallow pan stomach down and roast at 325°F for 6 to 6½ hours; a meat thermometer should read 185°F. (Always serve the fresh pork well done. There should be no tinge of pink.) During the roasting time, occasionally baste the roast with the butter drippings and the beer. For a crispy skin, spray the roast often with your plant mister.

Raisin Stuffing II
Nadzienie z Rodzynkami

3 egg yolks
2 tablespoons butter
¼ cup bread crumbs
salt and pepper to taste
¼ teaspoon cloves
1 tablespoon brown sugar
2 teaspoons parsley
2 teaspoons dill
¾ cup raisins
3 egg whites, beaten stiffly

Beat the egg yolks with the butter. Combine with all the other ingredients except the egg whites. Mix thoroughly. Finally, fold in the beaten egg whites and stuff the suckling pig as directed.

Fresh Peas with Dill Butter
Groszek z Masłem Koperkowym

3 cups water
1 teaspoon salt
4 pounds shelled peas

Bring the salted water to a boil, add peas, cover and simmer for 15 to 20 minutes. Drain, then serve dressed with dill butter.

Dill Butter

¼ pound unsalted butter
4 tablespoons chopped dill
1 teaspoon parsley

Melt butter slowly, then combine with the herbs. Pour over the peas and serve.

Peach Tarts and Plum Tarts
Brzoskwinie i Śliwki w Muszelkach z Ciasta

PLUM TARTS:
1 cup butter
2½ cups flour
1 cup confectioners sugar
2 teaspoons baking powder
2 eggs, beaten
3 tablespoons sour cream

Cut the butter into the flour, gradually adding the confectioners sugar and baking powder. Beat in the eggs and sour cream. Knead the dough, then chill for easier handling. Roll thin onto a greased cookie sheet. Cover the tin evenly with the dough.

TOPPING:
40 prune plums
1 cup confectioners sugar
2 tablespoons lemon juice

Slice the plums lengthwise, remove pits, and place on the dough, skin down, in even rows. Bake at 350°F for 45 to 50 minutes. While tarts cool, combine the confectioners sugar and lemon juice. Ice the cake and cut into 40 squares.

PEACH TARTS:

Use the same dough recipe as for the Plum Tarts.

15 fresh peaches, peeled and pitted
⅓ cup confectioners sugar

Slice the peaches in half and place, cut-side down, on dough in even rows. Bake at 350°F for 45 to 50 minutes. When cool, dust with confectioners sugar. Cut into 30 squares, allowing a peach half on each square.

SUMMER PARTY DINNER FOR 4

Herbed Tomato Salad / Sałatka Pomidorowa z Ziołami
Fresh Asparagus Omelet / Omlet ze Świeżych Szparagów
Flounder with Cauliflower / Flądra z Kalafiołem
Hot Buttered Rolls / Gorące Bułeczki z Masłem
Madeleines / Babeczki w Fartuszkach Papierowych

Make use of two of summer's finest vegetables, asparagus and cauliflower. The delicate tastes of these vegetables enhance the flavor of flounder. Round out the repast with a salad of vine-ripened tomatoes and crusty rolls, then finish off with madeleines for a light, unforgettable meal.

Herbed Tomato Salad
Sałatka Pomidorowa z Ziołami

4 ripe tomatoes
salt and pepper to taste
1 tablespoon chopped parsley
1 tablespoon fresh dill
3 tablespoons finely chopped chives
¼ cup freshly squeezed lemon juice
½ cup olive oil

Cut the tomatoes into thick slices. Combine the remaining ingredients in a bottle, shake well, and pour over the tomato slices. Allow salad to marinate in the refrigerator for an hour before serving.

Fresh Asparagus Omelet
Omlet ze Świeżych Szparagów

1 pound slender asparagus spears
6 eggs beaten
2 tablespoons milk
salt to taste
2 tablespoons butter

Use only the tender tips of the fresh asparagus (save stalks for soup). Slice into ½-inch pieces. Simmer for about 6 minutes in ½ cup water. Remove and drain. Beat the eggs with milk. Salt to taste. Melt butter in a very large skillet or omelet pan. Pour the egg mixture onto the butter and cook over low heat until the edges of the omelet begin to set. With a spatula, carefully bring the cooked portions at the edges toward the center, so the uncooked portions will flow to the bottom and set. Place the cooked asparagus spears on half the omelet, fold, and slide onto a heated platter. Cut into wedges and serve.

Flounder with Cauliflower
Flądra z Kalafiolem

1 cup sliced mushrooms
2 tablespoons butter
1½ pounds flounder fillets
⅔ cup boiling water
3 tablespoons flour
3 tablespoons butter
1 cup half-and-half
salt to taste
2 cups cooked cauliflower
½ teaspoon paprika
1 tablespoon chopped parsley

Sauté the mushroom slices in the butter. Place the fillets over the mushrooms, pour the boiling water over all, cover, and simmer for 15 minutes or until the fish begins to flake. Make a roux of the flour and butter, then gradually stir in the half-and-half. Salt to taste. Remove fillets to a warmed platter, then add the roux to the mushrooms and broth. Mix well. Arrange the heated cauliflower around the fillets. Spoon the sauce over all. Dust with the paprika, and garnish with parsley. Serve hot.

Besides being a decorative garnish, parsley is a surprisingly rich source of Vitamins A and C, calcium, niacin, riboflavin, and thiamin. Some afflicted herbalists are convinced that parsley tempers the pain of arthritis.

Madeleines

Babeczki w Fartuszkach Papierowych

1½ cups butter
4 eggs, beaten
1 cup sugar
2 teaspoons grated orange rind
1 teaspoon vanilla
1½ cups sifted flour
confectioners sugar

Clarify the butter by slowly melting it. Let stand (away from heat) until the clear liquid rises to the top and the solids settle to the bottom. Use a little of the clarified butter to grease the madeleine mold. Then lightly flour the mold.

In the top of a double boiler combine the eggs, sugar and orange rind. Cook over simmering water, beating until thick—about 5 minutes. Remove from heat. Add the vanilla and gradually stir in the flour. Finally pour in ¾ cup of the clarified butter. (Use the remaining clarified butter to grease the mold for later batches.) Mix well, then pour into the molds, filling each only half full. Bake at 350°F for 15 to 20 minutes. Cool, carefully loosen the madeleines from the molds and place on racks to cool completely. Wash, dry, grease and dust molds with flour before each use.

SUMMER LUNCH FOR 4

Summer's Potage / Potrawka Letnia
Mushroom Omelet Torte / Placek Omletowy z Grzybami
Potato Pancakes II / Placki Kartoflane
Creamed Spinach / Szpinak Przecierany
Strawberry Mousse / Mrożonka z Truskawek

This omelet should be an instant hit. Start with a frosty mug of Summer's Potage and top off the meal with regal Strawberry Mousse.

Summer's Potage
Potrawka Letnia

2 1-lb. cans sliced beets
1 tablespoon lemon juice
2 cups buttermilk
½ cup sour cream
salt to taste
1 small cucumber, peeled and quartered
1 hard-cooked egg, peeled and quartered
2 tablespoons chives

A Polish gazpacho! Place beets in blender, one can at a time. Blend until smooth. Blend remaining ingredients in a third whirl. Chill until frosty.

Mushroom Omelet Torte
Placek Omletowy z Grzybami

1 chopped onion
½ pound mushrooms, sliced
¼ cup butter
6 eggs, beaten
salt to taste
¼ cup grated cheese (optional)

Lightly sauté the onions and mushrooms in half the butter until the onions are transparent. Set aside on a warm platter. Using the remainder of the butter, make 2 omelets of the eggs and salt, in 2 separate skillets. When eggs are set, spoon the mushroom mixture onto one of the omelets, and cover it with the second, creating a sandwich effect. Garnish with grated cheese, if desired. Slice into quarters and serve immediately.

Potato Pancakes II
Placki Kartoflane

4 large potatoes, grated
1 large onion, minced
2 eggs
4 tablespoons sifted flour
salt to taste
½ cup bacon drippings

Mix first five ingredients well. Heat bacon drippings in a heavy skillet until almost smoking. Drop batter by spoonfuls into skillet. Flatten each pancake with a fork. Fry until golden on both sides (do not crowd).

Creamed Spinach
Szpinak Przecierany

¼ cup butter
¼ cup flour, sifted
1 cup light cream
garlic salt to taste
2 10-oz. packages frozen spinach, cooked and well
*   drained*

Make a roux of the butter and flour. Gradually whisk in the cream and season. Combine the sauce with the spinach. Warm through and serve immediately.
Note: For purists (or gardeners): instead of the frozen spinach, use 1½ pounds fresh spinach. Cover with boiling water and simmer for about 8 minutes. Drain and chop fine. Then proceed as directed above.

Strawberry Mousse
Mrożonka z Truskawek

1 quart strawberries, cleaned
⅓ cup sugar
⅔ cup wine
2 envelopes unflavored gelatin
½ cup cold water
½ cup boiling water
1 pint heavy cream

Hull the strawberries; reserve a few of the best for garnish; chop the rest of the berries with the sugar and wine in a blender. Soften the gelatin in cold water a few minutes, then add the boiling water, stir to dissolve. Combine the berry mixture with the gelatin and chill until thickened. Whip the heavy cream, and fold into the strawberry mixture.

Use plastic wrap to line a 2-quart mold. Spoon in the mouse. Chill overnight. Unmold and decorate with a few perfect strawberries.

SUMMER PICNIC FOR 4

Egg and Ham Roll-Ups / Krokiety z Jajek i Szynki
Turkey Platter with Mayonnaise Garnish /
Indyk w Przyprawie Majonezowej
Walnut Torte / Placek z Orzechów WΛoskich

Who wouldn't be beguiled by the idea of a magnificent picnic? The courses are all finger foods that can be served without fuss. The fun starts with Egg and Ham Roll-Ups for hors d'ouevre.

Egg and Ham Roll-Ups
Krokiety z Jajek i Szynki

8 hard-cooked eggs, shelled
16 thin ham slices
16 cherry tomatoes
salad greens

Slice eggs in half and roll each in a slice of ham. Place a cherry tomato on the top of each and secure with an hors d'ouevre pick. Serve on a bed of lettuce.

Turkey Platter with Mayonnaise Garnish
Indyk w Przyprawie Majonezowej

1 turkey breast
salt
juice of 1 lemon
3 carrots, peeled and chopped
3 onions, peeled and chopped
1 leek, chopped
1 celery root, finely chopped (optional)
3 celery stalks, chopped
1 bay leaf
salt and white pepper to taste

Rinse turkey breast and pat dry. Rub cavity with salt and drizzle lemon juice over the bird. Chill for several hours, then place in a large stockpot with the remaining ingredients, and water to cover. Simmer for 2½ hours, or until meat pulls easily from the bone. Skim as necessary. Remove turkey from the stock. (Save the stock with the cooked vegetables for another recipe for soup.)

Skin the bird and slice off the meat into serving pieces. Chill well. Arrange with the following garnish on a bed of salad greens:

> *1 cup cubed, jellied consommé*
> *1 cup cauliflowerets, cooked and drained*
> *3 hard-cooked eggs, peeled and sliced*
> *cherry tomatoes*
> *marinated mushrooms*
> *asparagus tips*
> *1 cup mayonnaise placed in a green pepper*
> *radish roses*

Mayonnaise (Blender Method)
Majonezem

1 egg
salt to taste
2 tablespoons cider vinegar
¼ teaspoon dry mustard
¼ teaspoon paprika
1 cup olive oil

Combine all ingredients except for the oil in the blender. While blender is running, gradually pour in the oil. Process until mayonnaise is thickened.

There are three basic varieties of paprika: the mild Spanish or Californian which are the most available on our supermarket shelves, and the Hungarian, which is slightly more difficult to obtain. It's well worth the extra effort, however, to find Hungarian paprika, which is more pungent. Polish recipes call for the Hungarian sweet variety known as the "noble rose" paprika. If you're only able to find one of the milder paprikas, you can add a little zip to it by combining a dash of chili powder or cayenne pepper with the paprika.

Walnut Torte

Placek z Orzechów Włoskich

12 egg yolks
1 cup sugar
½ pound walnuts, shelled and finely chopped
4 tablespoons flour, sifted
12 egg whites, beaten until peaks form

Combine the egg yolks with the sugar, nuts and flour, then fold in the egg whites. Grease and flour two 9 inch cake pans, then spoon mixture into pans. Bake at 325°F for 30 minutes. Remove from pans, let cool on racks, then sandwich the two layers together with this filling:

1 cup sugar
½ pound walnuts, shelled and finely chopped
¼ cup heavy cream

Mix the sugar and nuts; gradually stir in the cream. Use only enough cream to hold the filling together. If desired, drizzle some of the following icing over the top of the torte:

½ cup confectioners sugar
1 tablespoon lemon juice

Mix thoroughly and drizzle over the top of the torte.

Autumn Menus

There's a vicarious thrill that accompanies Autumn, as if one is on borrowed time before cold and snow approach. The invigorating, brisk mornings are warmed only by the golden colors of the leaves. Nature dons her most majestic plumage as she prepares to abdicate her sovereignty to King Boreas in a blaze of glory. When the autumnal winds finally become blustery, we gladly huddle around a steaming tureen of pungent soup or stew. Or, we exalt in the harvest bounty, gifts from the orchard and vineyard.

We band together against the fury of Winter's wrath in the security of a warm kitchen, reassured by an amply stocked pantry. We find solace in our cupboards that are brimming with preserves and homemade canned goods prepared during sunny bygone days. We're safe within the fortress of our hearth.

AUTUMN DINNER FOR 8

Green Pepper and Cauliflower Toss /
Sałatka z Papryki i Kalafiorów
Eggs "in the Shell" / Jajka Faszerowane
Savory Wild Goose / Smaczna Gęś Dzika
Fresh Peas with Tiny Onion Rings /
Groszek z Pierścieniami Drobnej Cebuli
Rice Pudding Garnished with Sour Cream Topping /
Budyń z Ryżu z Bitą Śmietaną

Eggs "in the Shell" is an ingenious method of serving diced, jazzed-up hard-cooked eggs in their own shells. They set the stage for Savory Wild Goose, an autumnal delicacy, accompanied by the Fresh Peas with Tiny Onion Rings. Top off the meal with Rice Pudding (topped by untraditional whipped *sour* cream).

Green Pepper and Cauliflower Toss
Sałatka z Papryki i Kalafiorów

1 small green pepper, chopped
1 small head of cauliflower, broken into flowerets
1 stalk celery, chopped
½ cup olive oil
juice of 1 lemon
salt and pepper to taste
lettuce leaves
dash paprika

Combine all ingredients but the lettuce leaves and paprika. Toss well, then arrange on the greens. Sprinkle with paprika.

Eggs "in the Shell"
Jajka Faszerowane

8 hard-cooked eggs, shells intact
4 tablespoons (½ stick) butter, softened
salt and pepper to taste
1 tablespoon fresh dill, chopped
½ cup grated cheese
paprika

Slice the eggs lengthwise with a sharp knife. Scoop out eggs and chop finely. (Save the shells.) Combine the eggs with all the ingredients except for the paprika. Restuff the shells with the mixture. Sprinkle with the paprika and place under the broiler until tops are browned. Serves 8.

Savory Wild Goose
Smaczna Gęś Dzika

1 goose (6 to 8 pounds)
salt
paprika
goose giblets, chopped
2 stalks celery, sliced
2 carrots, peeled and sliced
2 cups beef broth
1 onion, finely chopped
¼ cup goose fat (skimmed from drippings in roasting
    pan)
¼ cup flour
½ teaspoon marjoram
½ teaspoon thyme
1 cup sour cream
½ pound fresh mushrooms, sliced

Wash goose thoroughly. Salt and sprinkle with paprika. Place on rack in shallow pan. Roast, uncovered, at 350°F for 1½ hours.

During this time, simmer the giblets, celery and carrots in the beef broth. Then sauté the onion in the skimmed goose fat. Blend in the flour to make a roux, then gradually stir in the giblet broth, giblets, vegetables and spices. Slowly add the sour cream to the gravy mixture, stirring constantly to avoid curdling.

Remove goose from oven. Pour the gravy into a clean roasting pan with a lid. Place goose on top of gravy and sprinkle mushroom slices over gravy. Replace in oven, cover, and continue baking for another 2 hours. (This combination of roasting and braising makes the goose less fatty and ensures that it will be tender.)

Fresh Peas with Tiny Onion Rings
Groszek z Pierścieniami Drobnej Cebuli

> 2 *very small onions, thinly sliced*
> ¼ *pound butter*
> 2 *10-oz. packages frozen peas*
> ½ *teaspoon dill*

Sauté the onion slices in the butter. Cook the peas according to the directions on the package. Combine the peas with the onion/butter mixture, then garnish with the dill.

Rice Pudding Garnished with Sour Cream Topping
Budyń z Ryżu z Bitą Śmietaną

> 4 *cups cooked rice*
> ½ *cup sugar*
> ½ *teaspoon cinnamon*
> ½ *teaspoon nutmeg*
> 1 *cup seedless raisins*
> 4 *tablespoons butter*
> 4 *cups milk*
> 1 *teaspoon vanilla extract*

Combine all ingredients in a baking dish. Bake at 350°F for 30 minutes. Stir, then continue baking another 20 minutes, or until creamy and thick. Serve warm or chilled with this sour cream topping:

1 cup sour cream
1 teaspoon vanilla extract
⅓ cup sugar

Whip the cream until it peaks. Gradually whip in the vanilla and sugar. Mound the pudding (warm or chilled) in fancy bowls, and garnish with the sour cream topping.

AUTUMN BRUNCH FOR 4

September Salad / Sałata Wrześniowa
Polish Sausage Simmered in Wine /
Polska Kiełbasa Grzana w Winie
Scrambled Eggs Sprinkled with Chives /
Jajecznica ze Szczypiórkiem
Grilled Tomatoes / Pieczone Pomidory
Potato Croquettes / Knedle z Kartofli Duszonych i Mąki
Apple Raisin Cake / Placek z Jabłkowy z Rodzynkami

Enjoy the fruits of Autumn with September Salad, an intriguing medley of peaches, apples, tomatoes and cucumbers served on a bed of greens. Savor the Polish sausage which is simmered in red wine to bring out its flavors, and the subtle seasoning of chives to complement the eggs. Welcome the gifts of the orchard by baking this hearty and moist Apple Raisin Cake.

September Salad
Sałata Wrześniowa

2 *peaches, pitted, peeled and sectioned*
2 *apples, cored and sliced*
1 *tablespoon lemon juice*
2 *tomatoes, quartered*
1 *cucumber, sliced*
2 *tablespoons olive oil*
salt to taste
salad greens

Toss the peaches and apples in the lemon juice to prevent discoloration. Gently combine all the ingredients and arrange on the salad greens.

Polish Sausage Simmered in Wine
Polska Kiełbasa Grzana w Winie

1 *pound kielbasa*
1 *large onion, sliced*
2 *cups dry red wine (or enough to cover sausage)*

Simmer the sausage and onion in the wine over a low flame, covered, for 30 minutes. Lift from the wine, and slice on the bias about 1 inch thick. Arrange on a warmed platter.

Scrambled Eggs Sprinkled with Chives
Jajecznica ze Szczypiórkiem

8 eggs
¼ cup light cream (or half-and-half)
¼ cup butter
salt to taste
2 tablespoons minced fresh chives

Beat the eggs and cream together with a fork. Meanwhile, melt the butter slowly in a skillet—do not allow butter to brown. Pour egg mixture into the butter and stir until it sets. Turn onto warmed platter. Salt, if desired, and sprinkle with chives.

Grilled Tomatoes
Pieczone Pomidory

2 tomatoes
4 pats butter
1 tablespoon marjoram

Cut off ends of tomatoes and slice in halves. Place a pat of butter on top of each half, sprinkle with marjoram, and bake at 350°F for 10 minutes.

Potato Croquettes
Knedle z Kartofli Duszonych i Mąki

2 cups leftover mashed potatoes
2 eggs
½ cup flour
⅛ teaspoon nutmeg
1 egg, beaten
½ cup bread crumbs
4 tablespoons butter OR *enough fat for deep-frying*

Combine the first 4 ingredients. Roll mixture into a long rope. Cut into 3-inch links. Dip the links into the egg, then the bread crumbs. Fry in the butter or deep-fry in the fat until golden brown.

Apple Raisin Cake
Placek z Jabtkowy z Rodzynkami

1½ cups sugar
½ pound (2 sticks) butter, softened
4 eggs
1¾ cups flour
1 teaspoon cinnamon
½ teaspoon nutmeg
1 teaspoon baking soda
⅔ cup raisins
⅔ cup chopped walnuts
3 large apples, pared, cored and sliced

Cream the sugar and butter. Beat in the eggs, one at a time. Sift in the flour and spices into batter. Gradually add the remaining ingredients. Turn into a buttered and flour-dusted loaf pan and bake for 1 hour at 325°F, or until done. If desired, sprinkle with confectioners sugar just before serving.

AUTUMN SUPPER FOR 4

Raw Spinach and Pickled Egg Salad /
Sałatka ze Szpinaku z Kiszonymi Jajkami
Hunters' Stew / Gęsta Potrawka Myśliwska
Rye Bread with Sweet Butter / Żytni Chleb, na Słodkim
masle
Ice Cream / Lody
Almond Butter Cookies / Ciastka Migdałowe na Maśle

Begin the meal with a delectably colorful Raw Spinach
and Pickled Egg salad, then really dig into the Hunters'
Stew, a robust dish that satisfies the biggest appetite on
a chilly day. Devour this with an unusual round rye
bread spread with sweet butter. Then finish up with
homemade ice cream and Almond Butter Cookies.

Raw Spinach and Pickled Egg Salad
Salatka ze Szpinaku z Kiszonymi Jajkami

⅓ pound fresh spinach
1 small onion, sliced into rings
¼ cup fresh lemon juice
¼ cup olive oil
salt and pepper to taste
4 pickled eggs, sliced

Wash the spinach, drain and break into bite-sized pieces. Lightly toss with the onion rings. Combine the lemon juice, oil, salt and pepper and shake to mix. Set aside until just before serving. Garnish the salad with the pickled eggs. Drizzle the entire salad with the dressing and serve.

Pickled Eggs / Kiszone Jajka

2 cups beet juice
¼ cup sugar
¼ cup vinegar
4 eggs, hard-cooked

Combine the beet juice, sugar and vinegar and stir until dissolved and blended. Place peeled eggs in mixture, being sure the eggs are entirely covered with the juices. Allow to marinate overnight.

Hunters' Stew

Gęsta Potrawka Myśliwska

Hunters' Stew is an excellent recipe for using up left-overs. Each time you make this dish it should turn out different. Almost any combination of meats and vegetables is acceptable. It is one of Poland's most popular dishes.

>2 cups sauerkraut, rinsed
>½ pound Polish sausage, cut into bite-sized slices
>1 pound any leftover meat, preferably pork or beef
>1 cup bouillon or water
>½ cup red wine
>½ pound cabbage, sliced and cooked
>¼ pound bacon, diced
>½ pound fresh mushrooms
>2 small onions, chopped
>2 tablespoons flour
>2 tablespoons red wine
>2 tablespoons tomato paste
>salt to taste
>6 peppercorns
>½ cup red wine

Combine the first 5 ingredients, bring to a boil, then lower the heat and simmer for 2 hours. Add the cooked cabbage. Sauté the bacon, mushrooms and chopped onions. Stir in the flour, 2 tablespoons wine, tomato paste and seasonings. Combine this mixture with the meat and liquid mixture. Remove from heat and refrigerate overnight to allow the flavors to meld. To serve, reheat on top of the stove or in the oven (1 to 1½ hours at 350°F). Stir in the remaining ½ cup red wine just before serving.

Rye Bread
Żytni Chleb

2 cups buttermilk
½ teaspoon soda
¼ cup butter
salt to taste
1 teaspoon fennel seeds
1 tablespoon caraway seeds
⅔ cup molasses
⅓ cup water
1 envelope active dry yeast OR
  1 cake compressed yeast
3 cups all-purpose flour, sifted
3 cups rye flour
¼ cup melted butter
1 teaspoon caraway seeds

Combine the buttermilk and soda. Heat the next 6 ingredients in a saucepan. Bring to a boil, then immediately remove from heat and allow to cool to lukewarm. Dissolve the yeast in this lukewarm mixture. Pour the buttermilk into the yeast mixture and gradually sift the flours into this, mixing thoroughly all the time. Place on a lightly floured board and knead until smooth. Put dough in a greased bowl and allow to rise until doubled in bulk in a warm place (about 2 hours). Punch down, knead again, and separate into 2 balls. Place these on a lightly greased cookie sheet, brush with the melted butter, sprinkle with caraway seeds, and allow to rise again until doubled. Preheat oven to 350°F and bake for about 45 minutes, or until crust is lightly browned and crisp. Drizzle with butter again when removed from oven.

Vanilla Ice Cream
Lody

4 cups milk
⅓ cup flour
1½ cups honey
6 eggs, lightly beaten
1 to 1½ tablespoons vanilla extract
4½ cups heavy cream, whipped until it peaks

Using a double boiler, scald the milk, then dissolve the flour in it. Simmer until the mixture thickens, stirring constantly. Gradually stir in the honey, then the eggs, again constantly stirring. Allow mixture to cool before adding the vanilla and stiffly whipped cream. Freeze overnight, or until firm.

Almond Butter Cookies
Ciastka Migdałowe na Maśle

½ pound (2 sticks) butter, softened
2 cups flour
½ cup confectioners sugar
½ cup blanched and ground almonds

Thoroughly combine the butter and flour. Sift in the sugar and blend well. Add the almonds last and mix. Roll dough out thin and cut into shapes. Place on greased cookie sheet. Bake at 400°F for about 10 minutes, or until golden. Remove cookies immediately and allow to cool on a rack.

AUTUMN LUNCH FOR 4

Eggs Baked in Sea Shells /
Jajka Pieczone w Muszelkach Morskich
Hot Beet and Ripe Apple Relish /
Buraczki z Jabłkami na Gorąco
Pork Ribs and Cabbage / Żeberka Wieprzowe z Kapustą
Potatoes with Bacon Bits / Kartofle z Posiekaną Wędzonką
Chocolate Mazurek / Mazurek Czekoladowy

As the days begin to get blustery, it's soothing to be in an oven-warmed kitchen. The air is laden with the rich aromas of delicious stews bubbling in kettles or of confectionery marvels rising and browning in ovens. The juicy Pork Ribs and Cabbage is a cheery delight, especially when embellished by the Hot Beet and Ripe Apple Relish. The Eggs Baked in Sea Shells only sound and look exotic—they're really a snap to make. Drink in this homey atmosphere and linger over the meal with a wedge of rich chocolate mazurek (layer cake).

Eggs Baked in Sea Shells
Jajka Pieczone w Muszelkach Morskich

4 clean scallop shells (or ramekins)
4 pats of butter
4 eggs
salt to taste
¼ cup grated cheddar cheese
¼ cup buttered bread crumbs

Dot the center of each shell with the butter pat. Place in a 400°F oven until butter melts. Meanwhile combine the salt, cheese and bread crumbs. Remove shells from the oven, break an egg into each shell, then sprinkle the cheese/bread crumbs over each egg. Place in oven and bake until eggs are set (5 to 8 minutes).

Hot Beet and Ripe Apple Relish
Buraczki z Jabłkami na Gorąco

1 1-lb. can beets
2 apples, cored, peeled, sliced
2 tablespoons lemon juice
1 tablespoon sugar
salt to taste
½ cup sour cream
1 tablespoon flour

Combine first 5 ingredients in a blender and purée. Pour into a saucepan and heat gently. A few minutes before serving combine the sour cream and flour, then stir into the beet mixture. Mix and heat through. Do not boil.

Pork Ribs and Cabbage
Żeberka Wieprzowe z Kapustą

3 to 4 pounds ribs: pork spareribs or short ribs
¼ cup bacon drippings
6 peppercorns
salt to taste
1½ cups beef broth
¼ cup cider vinegar
1 carrot, diced
2 onions, chopped
¼ teaspoon caraway seeds
1 bay leaf
1 small head savoy cabbage, quartered

Brown the ribs in the bacon drippings. Season and combine with all the ingredients but the cabbage. Simmer for 1½ hours, adding more broth if necessary (keep meat covered). Add the cabbage quarters and continue cooking for another 30 minutes, or until cabbage is tender. Cut into serving pieces and arrange on heated platter with the cabbage.

Potatoes with Bacon Bits
Kartofle z Posiekaną Wędzonką

4 medium-sized potatoes, peeled
salt to taste
4 bacon strips, OR
   4 teaspoons prepared bacon bits
1 tablespoon minced onion
1 teaspoon snipped parsley

Cut potatoes into bite-sized pieces. Cook in salted water until tender. If using bacon strips, cut into pieces and sauté until crisp. Drain potatoes and combine with the cooked bacon and drippings or bacon bits and onion and parsley. Toss gently. Serve hot.

Chocolate Mazurek

Mazurek Czekoladowy

1 cup sugar
½ cup butter
½ cup melted baking chocolate
4 eggs, lightly beaten
1 teaspoon vanilla extract
salt to taste
1 tablespoon light cream, or milk
2 cups flour

White Icing
Grated nuts

Cream butter and sugar, then beat in the chocolate slowly. Add eggs, vanilla, salt and cream and mix well. Gradually sift in the flour. Spread evenly on a greased cookie sheet and bake at 350°F for 15 to 20 minutes. When cool, drizzle with the White Icing. Top with grated nuts of your choice.

White Icing

1 cup confectioners sugar
2 tablespoons rum or lemon juice

Combine ingredients well and drizzle over cake.

AUTUMN BRUNCH FOR 8

Radish / Escarole Bowl / Sałata Włoska z Rzodkiewką
Crêpes with Apple Filling / Naleśniki Nadziewane Jabłkami
Roast Pork with Apple Juice Glaze /
Pieczeń Wieprzowa z Glazurą Jabłecznikową
Buttered Baby Carrots / Marchewka na Maśle
Chilled Apricot Soup / Chłodnik Brzoskwiniowy

How about an afternoon outing at your local apple orchard? But first, arm yourself against the chills by hav-
ing a hot and hearty brunch. To help set the theme of
the day, enjoy festive Crêpes with Apple filling and
succulent Roast Pork with Apple Juice Glaze. For a
sweet conclusion, try one of the recipes for Chilled Apricot Soup.

Radish / Escarole Bowl
Sałata Włoska z Rzodkiewką

3 bunches escarole
3 bunches radishes, sliced (about 3 cups)
⅔ cup bacon bits

Wash escarole, drain and break into bite-sized pieces. Trim radishes and slice thinly. Use either ready-made bacon bits or fry 6 slices of bacon until crisp; drain, then crumble. Toss all ingredients together and dress with Sweet/Sour Dressing (see Index).

Crêpes with Apple Filling
Naleśniki Nadziewane z Jabłkami

3 eggs
1½ cups milk
1 cup flour
3 tablespoons sugar
salt to taste
2 tablespoons olive oil

Combine all ingredients thoroughly, then allow to "rest" for 1 to 1½ hours. Pour a small amount of batter onto a greased crêpe pan, tilting to allow batter to spread evenly. Brown lightly, remove and repeat until batter is used up. Fill crêpes with Apple Filling.

Apple Filling

4 apples
3 tablespoons butter
3 tablespoons apple juice or cider

Combine ingredients and simmer over low flame for about 20 minutes.

Roast Pork with Apple Juice Glaze
Pieczeń Wieprzowa z Glazura Jabłecznikową

1 fresh pork shoulder butt (about 4 pounds)
1 cup apple juice or cider
2 tablespoons brown sugar
1 apple (optional)
1 teaspoon lemon juice (optional)

Brown pork in its own fat in a Dutch oven. Combine apple juice (or cider) and brown sugar. Pour over roast and place in oven. Bake, uncovered, at 325°F for 3 to 3½ hours. Baste often. Serve with a garnish of fresh apple rings dipped in lemon juice.

Buttered Baby Carrots
Marchewka na Maśle

2 bunches baby carrots
½ cup butter
salt to taste
2 tablespoons sugar
½ cup vegetable broth

Wash carrots and snip off tops and tips. Combine all ingredients in a covered pan, over low heat, and braise until tender.

Chilled Apricot Soup
Chłodnik Brzoskwiniowy

EASY WAY:

2 1-lb. cans apricots, chilled and drained
1 teaspoon grated lemon rind
¾ cup sour cream

Pureé all ingredients in a blender, chill and serve.

TRADITIONAL WAY:

3 cups fresh apricots, not pitted
3 cups water
½ cup sugar, or to taste
1 tablespoon lemon juice
1 teaspoon grated lemon rind
2 tablespoons corn starch
¾ cup sour cream

Simmer the apricots in the water for ½ hour, or until very soft. Pit, then sieve. Combine the apricot pulp with the other ingredients, including the water that was used to cook the apricots, except the sour cream. Simmer until thickened, 5 to 10 minutes. Chill thoroughly and garnish each bowl with a dollop of sour cream.

AUTUMN DINNER FOR 4

Raw Spinach and Bacon Salad /
Sałatka ze Świeżego Szpinaku z Wędzonką
Venison Steaks in Wine Sauce /
Jelenie Bitki w Sosie Winnym
Cottage Style Eggs and Potatoes /
Jajka z Kartoflami po Wiejsku
Fresh Green Peas / Świeży Groszek Zielony
Cheesecake / Sernik

Hunters' delight! For those of you fortunate enough to have deer meat, Venison Steaks in Wine Sauce is a dish you will relish. For a bona fide meat and potatoes meal, serve Cottage Style Eggs and Potatoes, an uncommonly delicious marriage of flavors. Top off this hearty fare with a morsel of cheesecake. This particular cheesecake recipe is a scaled-down version of a complicated formula. You'll appreciate its simplicity.

Raw Spinach and Bacon Salad
Sałatka ze Świeżego Szpinaku z Wędzonką

> 1 *pound raw spinach*
> ⅔ *cup bacon bits*

Rinse spinach and drain. Break into bite-sized pieces. Use either ready-made bacon bits or fry 6 slices bacon until crisp; drain, then crumble. Toss the bacon bits with the spinach. Dress with Sweet/Sour Dressing.

Sweet/Sour Dressing

> ¼ *cup olive oil*
> ¼ *cup cider vinegar*
> 2 *tablespoons sugar*
> 2 *tablespoons water*
> *salt to taste*

Mix all the ingredients in a saucepan and bring to a boil. While still warm, pour over salad.

Venison Steaks in Wine Sauce

Jelenie Bitki w Sosie Winnym

¼ cup flour
4 steaks, cut from loin, about ¾-inch thick
1 onion, cut into rings
¼ cup butter
¼ teaspoon thyme
salt and pepper to taste
¼ pound fresh mushrooms, sliced
½ cup chablis or other dry white wine

Gently pound the flour into the steaks. Along with the onion rings, quickly brown the steaks in the butter over a high flame, in a Dutch oven. When steaks are browned on both sides, add the remaining ingredients, cover, and simmer over low heat (without peeking) for 20 minutes.

Cottage Style Eggs and Potatoes

Jajka z Kartoflami po Wiejsku

4 sliced, boiled potatoes
¼ cup butter
5 eggs
½ cup sour cream
salt and pepper to taste
2 tablespoons snipped chives

Sauté the potato slices in butter to a golden brown. Beat the eggs together with the sour cream. Gradually fold the eggs into the potatoes. Cook until set. Season. Turn out onto heated platter and shower with the snipped chives.

Cheesecake
Sernik

1 cup zwieback crumbs
2 8-oz. packages cream cheese, softened
1 teaspoon vanilla extract
5 egg whites
1 cup sugar
1 tablespoon grated lemon peel

Press zwieback crumbs onto the sides and bottom of a greased 8 inch springform pan. Cream the cheese and vanilla. Whip the egg whites and sugar until peaks form. Combine the cheese mixture with the meringue and lemon peel. Spoon into the crumb-lined pan. Bake at 350°F for 20 to 25 minutes. Allow cake to cook slowly on a rack, then place in refrigerator to chill for several hours.

AUTUMN CELEBRATION FOR 4

Deviled Eggs with Mushroom Bits /
Faszerowane Jajka z Grzybami
Cucumber Apple Salad / Mizeria z Ogórków i Jabłek
Grilled Tenderloin with Mushroom Caps /
Polędwica z Pieczarkami
Brussels Sprouts in Light Cheese Sauce /
Brukselka w Białym Sosie z Serem
Bread Pudding Topped with Whipped Sour Cream /
Chlebowy Budyń z Bitą Śmietaną

Indian Summer. Autumn and harvest are synonymous. Vegetables are abundant; hunting season is open. The menu is dictated by the wonderful eatables now available. Slice the cucumbers and apples paper-thin for this sublime salad. Then treat your palate to Grilled Tenderloin with Mushroom Caps, a luscious way of preparing beef filet with fluted mushrooms. (Save and chop the stems for the Deviled Eggs with Mushroom Bits.) Serve with Brussels sprouts garnished with a very subtle sauce. Complete the meal with Bread Pudding Topped with Whipped Sour Cream.

Deviled Eggs with Mushroom Bits
Faszerowane Jajka z Grzybami

4 hard-cooked eggs
salt to taste
2 tablespoons mayonnaise
¼ teaspoon dry mustard
2 tablespoons sautéed fresh mushrooms, chopped
paprika (optional)

Peel and halve the eggs, then place yolks in a bowl. Mash yolks with a fork until no lumps remain. Combine with all the ingredients but the paprika. Stuff the whites with the yolk mixture, and sprinkle tops with paprika.

Cucumber Apple Salad
Mizeria z Ogórków i Jabłek

2 cucumbers, sliced thin
2 apples, cored and sliced thin
4 radishes, sliced thin
3 tablespoons lemon juice
⅔ cup sour cream
2 teaspoons chopped dill
salt and pepper to taste

Place first 4 ingredients in a salad bowl, and toss, being sure to cover the apple slices completely with lemon juice. Season the sour cream and spoon over the salad just before serving.

The Poles are very fond of dill as a seasoning. However, in ancient herbal lore, it was considered to be a powerful charm against witchcraft. It's also said to cure ulcers.

Grilled Tenderloin with Mushroom Caps
Polędwica z Pieczarkami

4 4-oz. *tenderloin filets*
2 *tablespoons olive oil*
salt
freshly ground pepper to taste
¼ *pound fresh mushroom caps (save stems for the*
  Deviled Eggs)
2 *tablespoons butter*
2 *tablespoons mayonnaise*
1 *teaspoon horseradish*
4 *slices toast, crusts removed*

Brush the filets with oil and allow to marinate for several hours. Preheat the broiler, season the meat with salt and pepper, and grill under very high heat on both sides until meat reaches the desired degree of doneness. Meanwhile, gently sauté the mushrooms in butter. Combine the mayonnaise and horseradish and spread evenly on the toast. Place the toast on preheated plates, top the toast with the steaks, and spoon the mushrooms over all.

Brussels Sprouts in Light Cheese Sauce
Brukselka w Białym Sosie z Serem

1 *pound Brussels Sprouts*
1 *cup water salted to taste*
⅓ *cup grated cheddar cheese*
⅓ *cup butter, softened*
¼ *cup bread crumbs*

Clean and pick over Brussels sprouts. Cook the sprouts in the salted water about 10 to 15 minutes, or until tender. Drain. Blend the grated cheese with the softened butter. Place the Brussels sprouts in a heated bowl, spoon the cheese sauce over the sprouts, and sprinkle with bread crumbs.

Bread Pudding Topped with Whipped Sour Cream
Chlebowy Budyń z Bitą Śmietaną

6 egg yolks
½ cup sugar
1 cup pumpernickel bread crumbs
¼ teaspoon each nutmeg, cinnamon, cloves
3 tablespoons butter, melted
6 egg whites, whipped until peaks form
2 tablespoons white bread crumbs

Combine egg yolks and sugar. Stir in the pumpernickel crumbs, seasonings, and butter. Fold in the egg whites. Press the 2 tablespoons of bread crumbs into the sides and bottom of a greased cake pan. Pour the pudding mixture into the pan and bake at 325°F for 30 to 35 minutes. Serve warm with Whipped Sour Cream.

Whipped Sour Cream
Bita Śmietana

1 cup sour cream
1 teaspoon vanilla extract
¼ cup sugar

Combine ingredients and whip until smooth and stiff.

Winter Menus

A homey charm accompanies Winter. Families gather around the fireside and in the kitchen. Hot foods help warm the soul. These chilly days cry out for hearty food. Use this pleasurable season to draw friends and families closer together.

WINTER LUNCH FOR 4

Crêpes with Mushroom Filling /
Naleśniki z Nadzieniem Grzybowym
Chicken Livers Simmered in Madeira Sauce /
Watróbka Kurza Duszona w Sosie Madejra
Steamed Asparagus Tips /
Duszone Koniuszki Szparagowe
Brandied Peaches / Brzoskwinie Zaprawiane Gorzałką

This is an imposing meal that is achieved with a minimum of time and effort. Preparation time need only take 30 minutes. However, that can remain your secret. Let everyone marvel at your expertise.

Crêpes with Mushroom Filling
Naleśniki z Nadzieniem Grzybowym

1 cup milk
2 eggs
1 cup flour
salt to taste
2 tablespoons melted butter

Combine all ingredients thoroughly, then allow to "rest" for 1 to 1½ hours. Pour a small amount of batter onto a greased crêpe pan, tilting to allow batter to spread evenly. Brown lightly, remove the crêpe to a warmed platter and repeat until batter is used up.

Mushroom Filling

1 pound sliced mushrooms
1 onion, chopped fine
½ cup butter, or as needed
pepper and salt to taste
1 tablespoon chopped parsley
2 tablespoons bread crumbs OR
    1 tablespoon flour
4 tablespoons sour cream

Sauté the mushrooms and onion in the butter. Season. Stir in the parsley and the bread crumbs or flour. Allow the mixture to simmer over low heat for 10 minutes, or until mixture binds. Place 2 or 3 tablespoons filling onto each crêpe and roll up. Garnish with sour cream.

Chicken Livers Simmered in Madiera Sauce
Watróbka Kurza Duszona w Sosie Madejra

1 pound chicken livers
1 cup milk
1 onion, chopped fine
¼ cup butter
½ cup flour
1 cup chicken broth
½ cup Madeira wine
salt and pepper to taste
parsley (optional)

Soak livers in milk overnight. (Cats will love the discarded milk in the morning.) Gently sauté the onion until translucent. Flour the chicken livers heavily and lightly brown in the onion and butter. Turn the heat to low, add the broth and wine and simmer for 20 minutes. Correct seasonings and garnish with parsley, if desired.

Steamed Asparagus Tips
Duszone Koniuszki Szparagowe

1 pound asparagus
salted boiling water to cover
¼ cup butter

Wash asparagus and remove tough ends by breaking off. Scrape off scales and rinse well. Place in shallow pan, cover with the boiling, salted water and cook over high heat for 15 minutes, or until tender when pierced with a fork. Drain, dot with butter and serve immediately.

Brandied Peaches

Brzoskwinie Zaprawiane Gorzałką

4 peaches
1 cup marmalade OR
peach preserves
½ cup brandy

Peel peaches, halve, and remove pit. Place rounded-side-up in an elegant baking dish. Spoon marmalade over peach halves and sprinkle with brandy. Cover and bake for 15 minutes at 350°F.

CHRISTMAS EVE DINNER FOR 4 OR 8

Christmas Eve Barszcz / Barszcz Wigilijny
Christmas Almond Soup / Wigilijna Zupa Migdałowa
Beer Soup with Eggs / Piwna Zupa z Jajkami
Smoked Salmon Omelets / Omlety z Wędzonym Łososiem
Poached Pike / Gotowany Szczupak na Gorąco
Carp with Horseradish Sauce / Karp w Sosie Chrzanowym
Baby Carrots Polonaise / Marchewka po Polsku
Hot Polish Chicory / Polska Cykoria na Gorąco
Mushroom Stuffed Tomatoes /
Pomidory Nadziewane Grzybami
Christmas Eve Bread / Chleb Wigilijny
Poppyseed Roll / Makownik Zawijany
Fruit Compote / Kompot Owocowy

Christmas Eve is a quiet, tradition-steeped time with deep religious significance. No meat is served since Christmas Eve is a fast day. However, this meal traditionally is an elaborate one of many courses. There are always three different soups, one of course being barszcz. Also numbered among the foods are three fish entrées including pike or carp. There must be an odd number of appetizers, garnishes, accompaniments, and desserts to complete the meal.

Even the most diligent chef finds it difficult to incorporate all the above dishes in one meal. All of the recipes are included, so, choose a fine sampling of what most suits your own needs or what won't overburden your already groaning table. Most of these recipes are for 4 people but can easily be doubled or tripled to feed homecoming family and friends.

147

Christmas Eve Barszcz

Barszcz Wigilijny

1 onion, chopped
2 stalks celery, sliced
2 carrots, peeled and chopped
¼ head savoy cabbage
salt and pepper to taste
6 cups beef broth
6 fresh beets, OR
    1 can red beets, chopped
sugar to taste
2 teaspoons lemon juice

Combine the first 6 ingredients and simmer for 40 minutes. (If using fresh beets, wash and bake at 350°F for 40 minutes. Then peel, chop fine and add to the other vegetables.) Stir in sugar. Simmer for 10 minutes. Sprinkle with lemon juice and serve.

Christmas Almond Soup

Wigilijna Zupa Migdałowa

4 cups milk
½ pound almonds, finely ground
2 cups cooked, leftover rice
1 teaspoon almond extract
½ cup currants or raisins
3 tablespoons sugar, or to taste

Combine all ingredients, and heat through gently. Don't scald the milk. Serve after the fish course.

Beer Soup with Eggs
Piwna Zupa z Jajkami

8 egg yolks (use egg whites for another recipe)
1 or 2 tablespoons honey
6 12-oz. cans beer

Beat the yolks and honey until frothy. Heat beer to boiling. Add a spoonful of beer to the egg mixture and beat. Continue adding small amounts of beer to the eggs, then combine and beat vigorously to avoid curdling. Serve at once.
Note: This recipe serves 8.

Smoked Salmon Omelets
Omlety z Wędzonym Łososiem

8 eggs
¼ cup milk
salt to taste
2 tablespoons butter
4 1-oz. slices smoked salmon

Beat eggs with milk and salt with a whisk and pour into a hot frying pan or omelet pan containing the melted butter. Lift cooked portions of the omelet with a fork to allow uncooked portions to flow to the bottom of the pan. Avoid stirring. Tilt pan to hasten the flow to the sides and bottom of pan, but return to level cooking position to ensure uniform thickness of omelet. When bottom is light brown, gently lift out onto a warm plate and top with salmon slices. Cut into quarters and serve at once.

Poached Pike
Gotowany Szczupak na Gorąco

4 pounds pike
court bouillon (see below)
½ cup butter
4 tablespoons lemon juice
1 tablespoon flour
2 cups sour cream
salt and pepper to taste
fresh chopped dill (optional)

Rinse the fish well. Place as many fish as will easily fit onto the bottom of a deep pot. Several batches may have to be poached. Cover with the court bouillon, bring to a boil, then promptly remove, while still only partially done. Remove cautiously with a spatula, taking care not to let the fish fall apart. Place in a baking dish, dot with butter, and sprinkle with lemon juice. Combine the flour with the sour cream, and smother the pike with this mixture. Bake at 300°F for about 20 minutes, continually basting with the sauce. Season and garnish with dill, if desired.
Note: This recipe serves 8.

Court Bouillon

1 quart water
2 cups white wine
1 heaping teaspoon salt
1 onion, coarsely chopped
2 carrots, coarsely chopped
3 bay leaves
1 lemon, sliced, and studded with whole cloves

Combine all ingredients, bring to a boil, and simmer for 1 hour before using to poach fish.

Carp with Horseradish Sauce
Karp w Sosie Chrzanowym

The flavor of carp is better when the fish is taken from cold waters, the best season being from October through March. The firm-fleshed fish is a true delicacy when prepared with care. Besides being sold whole, it's also marketed as fillets, steaks, and is occasionally smoked.

1 carp (4 pounds) cut in serving pieces
2 cups cold water
½ cup vinegar
⅔ cup flour
½ cup melted butter
1 cup white wine

Horseradish Sauce

1 tablespoon grated, fresh horseradish OR
*   2 tablespoons prepared horseradish*
2 beaten egg yolks
1 tablespoon chopped chives
salt and pepper to taste

Rinse the carp pieces in the water/vinegar solution. Wipe gently with a damp cloth, then dredge the pieces in flour. Sauté over medium heat in the butter. Lightly brown on both sides, then add the wine. Cover and simmer for 10 to 15 minutes, stirring occasionally.

Gently remove fish to a heated serving dish. Gradually add the egg yolks and horseradish to the pan drippings. Heat until blended and slightly thickened. Correct seasoning. Spoon the sauce over the fish, sprinkle with chives, and serve immediately.
Note: This recipe serves 8.

Baby Carrots Polonaise
Marchewka po Polsku

1 pound baby carrots, well scrubbed
1 cup water
salt to taste
sugar to taste
2 tablespoons butter, melted
2 tablespoons bread crumbs

Simmer the carrots in seasoned boiling water for 10 to 15 minutes, or until tender. Drain and place in serving dish. Combine the butter and bread crumbs, and crumble over the carrots.

Hot Polish Chicory
Polska Cykoria na Gorąco

4 heads chicory
1 cup water
salt and pepper to taste
½ tablespoon vinegar
½ cup butter
2 hard-cooked eggs, sieved or chopped
chopped parsley

Wash the chicory and remove the bitter centers. Boil the water with the salt, pepper and vinegar. Reduce heat, add the chicory and simmer for 10 to 15 minutes. Drain. Brown the butter in a hot skillet. Arrange chicory on a warmed platter. Drizzle the browned butter over the chicory heads. Garnish with the sieved eggs and parsley.

Mushroom Stuffed Tomatoes
Pomidory Nadziewane Grzybami

4 large, firm tomatoes
¼ pound fresh mushrooms, chopped
2 tablespoons butter
2 tablespoons bread crumbs
2 tablespoons sour cream
salt to taste
white pepper to taste

Slice tops off tomatoes, and scoop seeds out. Sauté the mushrooms and onion in butter lightly (5 to 10 minutes) then combine with the bread crumbs, sour cream and seasonings. Stuff the tomatoes, replace the tomato tops, place in a shallow, greased pan, and bake for 25 to 30 minutes at 350°F.

Christmas Eve Bread
Chleb Wigilijny

This traditional Polish Christmas Eve fare is somewhat similar to fruitcake.

2 cups confectioners sugar
6 eggs
½ pound (2 sticks) butter, softened
¼ cup vodka
2 teaspoons grated lemon peel
1 teaspoon vanilla extract
2½ cups flour, sifted
2 teaspoons baking powder
¾ cup seedless raisins
⅔ cup walnuts, chopped
½ cup candied orange peel pieces, either prepared, or
  homemade (see Index)

Whip the sugar with the eggs, then gradually add the butter. Beat in the vodka, lemon peel, and vanilla. Slowly sift in the flour, and baking powder. Stir in the remaining ingredients. Pour the batter into a greased and floured 9½×5×3-inch loaf pan, and bake at 350°F for 55 to 60 minutes. Cool in pan 10 minutes; remove to cooling rack.

Poppyseed Roll

Makownik Zawijany

1 package active dry yeast
4 ounces warm water
4 ounces light cream or half-and-half
2 tablespoons sugar
1 teaspoon salt or to taste
1 egg, beaten
3 cups flour, sifted
2 tablespoons melted butter
2 cans poppyseed filling
2 tablespoons melted butter

Allow yeast to soften in the warm water. Scald the light cream, remove from heat, and add the sugar and salt. When cooled, blend in the yeast and egg. Gradually sift in the flour, and mix well. Stir in the butter, and, if necessary, add a bit more flour to form a medium-firm dough. Knead for several minutes, until smooth. Place dough in a greased bowl, cover, and let rise until doubled in bulk, about 1 hour. Punch down, then roll dough into a rectangle. Spread the poppyseed filling evenly and roll up as you would a jelly roll. Place on a well-buttered cookie sheet. Cover and allow to rise again until doubled in size. Drizzle melted butter over the top and bake for 30 to 35 minutes at 375°F. If desired, you may glaze the roll while still warm with the following glaze:

> 1 cup confectioners sugar
> 2 tablespoons lemon juice

Fruit Compote

Kompot Owocowy

> 1 cup dried fruit
> 2 cups water
> ¾ cup sugar
> 1 stick cinnamon
> 3 whole cloves
> 2 tablespoons grated lemon rind
> 1 tablespoon lemon juice

Allow the fruit to plump up by soaking it overnight in the water. Add the remaining ingredients and heat until the sugar is dissolved. Chill for several hours, remove the cinnamon and cloves, and enjoy.

WINTER LUNCH FOR 4

Cabbage, Leek and Orange Salad /
Sałata z Kapusty, Porów i Pomarańczy
Bisque of Potato Soup with Bacon /
Gęsta Zupa Kartoflana z Wędzonką
Miniature Meat Patties / Sznycelki w Cieście
Eggs Baked with Bechamel Sauce /
Jajka Wypiekane w Białym Sosie
Honey Almond Cookies / Pierniczki z Migdałami

This robust combination of foods provides an ideal anti-dote for a shivery winter day, and does so with a certain flair. Start with a bowl of creamy Bisque of Potato Soup with Bacon, then have an original salad that contains your minimum daily requirement of Vitamins A, B, C and D. Progress to the Miniature Meat Patties that are patterned in an enchanting pinwheel fashion. Bake your eggs with bechamel sauce right along with the entrée. Finally savor the Honey Almond Cookies with pots of steaming coffee.

Cabbage, Leek and Orange Salad
Sałata z Kapusty, Porów i Pomarańczy

2 cups shredded red cabbage
2 oranges, peeled and cut in segments
½ cup finely chopped leek
2 tablespoons lemon juice
⅓ cup olive oil
2 tablespoons honey

Toss the first 3 ingredients well. Then combine the lemon juice, oil and honey. Toss the dressing and cabbage mixture together and allow the flavors to blend for one hour.

Bisque of Potato Soup with Bacon
Gęsta Zupa Kartoflana z Wędzonką

4 small potatoes, peeled and sliced
1 carrot, peeled and sliced
2 cups vegetable or chicken broth
1 small minced onion
3 strips bacon, chopped
1 tablespoon flour
salt to taste
1 cup milk
1 teaspoon chopped parsley

Simmer the potatoes and carrot in the broth until tender. Sauté the onion with the bacon. When lightly browned, stir in the flour and the salt. Gradually add the milk, stirring constantly. Combine the two mixtures and purée in the blender, a cupful at a time. Garnish with parsley.

Miniature Meat Patties
Sznycelki w Cieście

FILLING:

½ pound ground pork
1 tablespoon butter
2 tablespoons water
1 small minced onion
¼ cup finely chopped mushrooms
salt to taste
1 teaspoon parsley

Thoroughly brown the pork in the butter. Add the remaining ingredients and simmer for 1 hour.

TRADITIONAL PASTRY DOUGH:

1½ cups flour
3 tablespoons butter
2 tablespoons sour cream
1 egg
1 egg yolk
1 teaspoon baking powder
1 egg white, lightly beaten

Combine flour and butter completely. Gradually add all the remaining ingredients except for the egg white. Knead the dough, then roll out on a floured board into a long rectangle. Spread filling evenly over the dough, then roll up jelly-roll fashion. Brush top of dough with the egg white. Slice into 12 patties. Bake on a greased cookie sheet at 375°F for 25 to 30 minutes.

EASY PASTRY DOUGH:

Use a package of refrigerated crescent roll dough. Separate into the triangles, spread with the filling, roll up, and bake according to the directions on the package.

Eggs Baked with Bechamel Sauce
Jajka Wypiekane w Białym Sosie

4 hard-cooked eggs, shelled and halved
2 tablespoons butter
2 tablespoons flour
1 cup light cream
salt to taste
¼ teaspoon lemon juice
1 egg yolk, beaten
paprika

Place the eggs, flat side down, into a buttered casserole dish. Make a roux of the butter and flour. Gradually, pour in the cream, stirring constantly. When thickened, remove from heat. Add the salt, lemon juice, and egg yolk. (Mix 3 tablespoons of the white sauce into the egg-yolk mixture, then, when well blended, stir the egg mixture into the rest of the sauce.) Spoon over the hard-cooked eggs, sprinkle with paprika, and bake at 375°F for 10 to 15 minutes.

Honey Almond Cookies
Pierniczki z Migdałami

1 cup honey
3 eggs
3 cups sifted flour
1 teaspoon baking soda
½ teaspoon nutmeg
½ teaspoon ginger
½ teaspoon cinnamon
2 egg whites
blanched almond halves

Combine honey and eggs thoroughly. Add flour, soda and spices and mix well. Press mixture into a ball and refrigerate for several hours until stiff. Roll out on floured surface to about ¼-inch thick and cut with a floured glass or round cookie cutter. Lightly brush tops of cookies with egg whites and press a nut into each. Bake on greased cookie sheets at 350°F for about 15 minutes.

WINTER DINNER FOR 4

Chilled Eggs and Medley of Fresh Vegetables /
Zimne Jajka i Wybór Świeżych Jarzyn
Roast Duck Served with Red Cabbage /
Pieczona Kaczka z Czerwoną Kapustą
Mashed Potatoes / Duszone Ziemniaki
Orange Butter Cake / Pomarańczowy Placek na Maśle

The Grand Slam. Open the bidding with an antipasto of Chilled Eggs and Medley of Fresh Vegetables. Use your imagination to create a different combination each time you serve it. Pass the succulent Roast Duck with Red Cabbage. They'll double their bid for more. However, the Ace of Trumps is the Orange Butter Cake. I'll wager your guests would like to have another piece of the "action".

Chilled Eggs and Medley of Fresh Vegetables
Zimne Jajka i Wybór Świeżych Jarzyn

Arrange peeled hard-cooked egg halves and fresh, artfully cut vegetables, such as cauliflowerettes, carrot curls, cherry tomatoes, radish roses, etc., on crisp greens. Use your imagination to create a different medley each time. Serve with homemade mayonnaise or your favorite dressing or dip.

Roast Duck with Red Cabbage
Pieczona Kaczka z Czerwoną Kapustą

1 young duck
salt
2 onions, peeled and quartered
2 apples, pared and quartered
3 strips bacon
1 cup water

Rinse and dry the bird and rub the inside of the cavity with salt. Stuff duck with the onions and apples. Place the bird breast side up on a rack in a roasting pan. Secure bacon strips on top to keep the duck breast moist. Add the water to the roaster, and baste the bird often. Bake at 325°F 20 minutes per pound. Discard onions and apples. Mound the red cabbage onto a heated platter. Carve the duck into serving pieces, and arrange over the cabbage. Serve immediately.

CABBAGE MIXTURE:

¼ pound bacon, sliced
1 medium-sized red cabbage
1 onion, minced
½ cup red wine
¼ cup lemon juice

Brown the bacon; add to it the cabbage, onion, wine and lemon juice. Cover and simmer for 15 minutes.

Orange Butter Cake

Pomarańczowy Placek na Maśle

⅓ cup butter
⅔ cup sugar
3 tablespoons orange rind, grated
1½ cups flour, sifted
1½ teaspoons baking powder
3 tablespoons orange juice

Cream the butter and sugar. Gradually beat in the remaining ingredients. Pour batter into a greased and floured 9½ × 5 × 3-inch loaf pan. Bake for 40 minutes at 350°F. Cool, then frost.

FROSTING:

2 cups confectioners sugar
3 tablespoons butter, softened
2 tablespoons orange juice

Cream the butter and sugar. Add the juice, a little at a time.

WINTER PARTY DINNER FOR 4

Winter's Seasonal Salad / Sałata na Sezon Zimowy
Layered Eggs and Vegetable Casserole /
Jajka Zapiekane z Jarzyną
Pork Steaks Simmered in Red Wine Sauce /
Kotlety Wieprzowe, Duszone w Czerwonym Winie
Vanilla Cream Mold / Galareta z Lodów Waniliowych

The recipe for Pork Steaks Simmered in Red Wine Sauce will warm and cajole your pálate. It's the gentle simmering that fuses their delicate flavors. Accompany this royal fare with Layered Eggs and Vegetable Casserole baked to a golden perfection. Crown the meal with shimmering Vanilla Cream Mold.

Winter's Seasonal Salad
SaƗata na Sezon Zimowy

fresh spinach leaves
lettuce leaves
1 onion, sliced
radish roses

Toss together, then drizzle with the following dressing:

½ cup olive oil
¼ cup vinegar
garlic salt to taste
¼ teaspoon paprika
snipped parsley

Combine all ingredients in a bottle and shake until well blended.

Layered Eggs and Vegetable Casserole
Jajka Zapiekane z Jarzyną

2 minced onions
½ pound mushrooms, sliced
3 tablespoons butter
5 hot, boiled, sliced potatoes
5 hot, hard-cooked eggs, peeled and sliced
½ teaspoon sweet basil
salt and pepper to taste
¼ cup white wine
½ cup sour cream
1 teaspoon flour
parsley (optional)

Gently sauté the onions and mushrooms in the butter. In a greased casserole dish, make four layers in this order: 1) sliced potatoes, 2) onions and mushrooms, 3) sliced eggs, covered by another 4) layer of potatoes. Season each layer with a dash of sweet basil, salt and pepper. Combine the wine, sour cream, and flour and spoon over the top layer of potatoes. Garnish with parsley and bake at 400°F for 15 minutes.

Aside from being an indispensible additive to many dishes, basil is purported to relieve headaches and to soothe the stomach.

Pork Steaks Simmered in Red Wine Sauce

Kotlety Wieprzowe, Duszone w Czerwonym Winie

4 boneless pork loin steaks
3 tablespoons vegetable oil
1 cup minced onion
1 cup mushrooms, sliced
1 tablespoon raisins
⅛ teaspoon cinnamon
1 cup red wine

Brown the steaks in oil, then remove from skillet. Sauté the onion and mushrooms until golden in the drippings. Return the steaks to the pan, add the remaining ingredients, cover, and simmer for an hour or more.

Vanilla Cream Mold

Galareta z Lodów Waniliowych

1 pint whipping cream
2 teaspoons vanilla extract
⅔ cup sugar
2 teaspoons cornstarch
⅓ cup milk
¼ cup sugar

Heat the cream, vanilla, and sugar to just below the boiling point. (Boiling will curdle the cream.) Stir constantly. Blend the cornstarch and milk, then stir into the cream. Dampen the inside of a 1-quart mold with water, then evenly distribute the ¼ cup sugar in it. Keep the cream hot until it begins to thicken, then pour into the sugar-lined mold. Chill overnight. Unmold. If desired, serve with blueberry preserves.

WINTER BRUNCH FOR 4

Apple / Beet / Cabbage Salad /
Sałatka z Jajek, Buraków i Kapusty
Shirred Eggs / Jajka Wypiekane w Śmietanie
Baked Polish Ham / Polska Szynka Pieczona
Cherry Dumplings / Knedle Wiśniowe
Orange Glazed Apples / Jabłka w Glazurze Pomarańczowej

Enjoy this leisurely brunch of winter fruits and simple dishes. The meal practically makes itself. A blender or processor shreds the salad in no time. The Shirred Eggs and Baked Polish Ham take care of themselves in the oven. The Cherry Dumplings take only 15 minutes to make. (Honest!) Ditto for the equally appealing Orange Glazed Apples. Rather than fussing or fuming in the kitchen, lavishly spend your time with your guests and family.

Apple / Beet / Cabbage Salad

Sałatka z Jajek, Buraków i Kapusty

2 cups shredded cabbage
1 cup finely sliced pickled beets
2 cups cored, chopped apples
⅓ cup vinegar
½ cup olive oil
outer cabbage leaves (optional)
chopped parsley (optional)

A blender or food processor saves time with the shredding and chopping. Combine the first 5 ingredients and toss well. If desired, serve in a chilled salad bowl which is lined with cabbage leaves. Garnish with chopped parsley.

Shirred Eggs

Jajka Wypiekane w Śmietanie

8 eggs
4 pats butter
4 tablespoons light cream
salt to taste

Preheat oven to 400°F. Into each of 4 individual ramekin, place a pat of butter. Place ramekins in oven until butter melts. Break 2 eggs into each ramekin, add 1 tablespoon cream and salt and replace in oven. Bake about 8 minutes, (12 minutes if using 1 large casserole instead of individual dishes.) or just until egg whites are set. Serve immediately.

Baked Polish Ham
Polska Szynka Pieczona

A really fine Polish ham needs no sauce. Just reheat (a fully cooked ham) and serve!

Cherry Dumplings
Knedle Wiśniowe

4 tablespoons bread crumbs
3 tablespoons butter
2 egg yolks
½ cup milk
1 cup flour
salt to taste
½ pound morello cherries
4 tablespoons melted butter
4 tablespoons sugar

Combine bread crumbs, butter, egg yolks and milk to form a paste. Mix in flour and salt. Shape into tiny dumplings, and insert 2 cherries into center of each. Drop into a deep pot of boiling water, and cook for about 5 minutes, or, until they rise to the top. Drain and serve, topped with butter and sugar.

Orange Glazed Apples
JabƚKa w Glazurze Pomarańczowej

4 apples
2 teaspoons grated orange rind
½ cup orange juice
½ cup honey
1 tablespoon butter

Do not peel, but core and quarter the apples. Set aside. Combine remaining ingredients and simmer for 10 minutes. Add the apples to the glaze; turn to glaze evenly. Cover, and cook for 10 minutes, or more. Serve hot!

WINTER SUPPER FOR 4

Crunchy Apple Carrot Salad /
Chrupiąca Sałatka z Jabłek i Marchewki
Cucumber in Sour Cream Relish /
Ogórki w Przyprawie z Kwaśnej Śmietany
Cabbage Roll-Ups / Gołąbki Mięsne z Ryżem
Eggplant Crisps / Kruchy Placek z Bakłażanów
Cream Puff Pie /
Placek z Kwaśnej Śmietany i Żółtek pod Pianą z Białek

Here's a popular Polish treat that should be an instant hit with your crowd. Try Cabbage Roll-Ups, a zesty creation of a meat filling, wrapped in cabbage leaves, then baked in a tomato sauce. Add some crisp condiments and accompaniments, such as Crunchy Apple Carrot Salad, and Cucumbers in Sour Cream Relish. Munch on some Eggplant Crisps, then consume the feathery Cream Puff Pie for the climax of a memorable feast.

Crunchy Apple Carrot Salad
Chrupiąca Sàłatka z Jabłek i Marchewki

4 carrots, peeled and grated
2 apples, cored and chopped
½ cup sour cream
1 tablespoon horseradish
salt to taste
1 tablespoon sugar
1 tablespoon lemon juice

Combine all ingredients, being sure to coat the apples thoroughly to avoid discoloration. Serve immediately. Garnish with carrot curls, if desired.

Cucumber in Sour Cream Relish
Ogórki w Przyprawie z Kwaśnej Śmietany

salt
2 cucumbers, peeled and sliced very thin
1 small onion, sliced very thin
1 teaspoon minced fresh dill
⅔ cup sour cream
1 tablespoon vinegar

Salt cucumber slices and allow to drain for 45 minutes. Mix all ingredients and serve.

Cabbage Roll-Ups
Gołąbki Mięsne z Ryżem

1 pound ground pork
1 pound ground beef

1 onion, minced
½ cup butter
2 cups cooked rice
1 tablespoon chopped fresh dill
salt and pepper to taste
10 cabbage leaves
1 large can spaghetti sauce

Sauté meats and onion in butter; blend in the rice and seasonings. Boil 10 large cabbage leaves (1 or 2 at a time) for 1 minute. Drain, then place some of the meat mixture in the center of each leaf. Fold edges over and place open side down in a greased casserole dish. Pour sauce over all and bake at 350°F for 35 to 40 minutes.

Eggplant Crisps

Kruchy Placek z Bakłażanów

1 eggplant (about 1 pound), peeled
¾ cup flour
salt and pepper to taste
2 tablespoons milk
2 eggs, beaten
1 cup dry bread crumbs
1 cup oil, or as needed

Slice eggplant lengthwise into ¾-inch pieces. Cover eggplant strips with cold water and allow to set for 30 minutes. Drain. Mix the flour, salt and pepper. In another bowl beat the milk into the eggs. Dredge eggplant strips in the seasoned flour, dip in the egg mixture, roll in the bread crumbs, then fry in the oil until crisp and golden.

Cream Puff Pie

Placek z Kwaśnej Śmietany i Żółtek pod Piana z Białek

PASTRY:

2 cups sifted flour
2 teaspoons sugar
1 teaspoon salt
1 cup shortening
4 to 5 tablespoons icy water

Sift the first 3 ingredients together. Cut the shortening into the flour until the mixture looks like rice kernels. Sprinkle water over all and toss with a fork until mixture is evenly dampened. Press into a ball, then roll out on a floured surface.

FILLING:

5 egg yolks
⅓ cup sugar
2 tablespoons grated lemon rind
1 cup sour cream
¼ cup flour
5 egg whites

Beat egg yolks and sugar together. Blend in everything else but the egg whites. Whip the egg whites until stiff, then fold into the egg-yolk mixture. Line a 9-inch pie pan with the pastry. Spoon filling mixture into unbaked piecrust, then cover with the top (unbaked) crust. Pinch edges together. Bake in 350°F oven for 30 to 40 minutes. Sprinkle with extra sugar, if desired.

Vodka

A man of the working classes who wants to celebrate payday will drink vodka straight up. It is also the accompaniment to the finest of caviars. Poland has never experienced prohibition—alcohol has never become a moral issue. There are unlimited methods for flavoring vodka, all easy and imaginative. Try one or more of the following.

VODKA BEVERAGES
NAPOJE Z WÓDKI

Iced Coffee Polish Style
Kawa Mrożona po Polsku

½ cup sugar
5 cups chilled, strong coffee
1 cup vanilla ice cream
½ cup vodka
2 cups whipped heavy cream

Blend sugar with coffee and refrigerate for several hours. Distribute ice cream equally among 4 glasses. Splash with vodka, add the sweetened coffee and top with the whipped cream. Serves 4.

Iced Coffee with Vodka
Kawa Mrożona z Wódką

5 cups chilled strong coffee
½ cup sugar or honey
½ cup vodka

Combine ingredients and chill to blend. Serve over crushed ice. Serves 4.

Summer Punch
Poncz Letni

3 oranges, peeled and mashed
3 cups sugar
1 sliced orange
1 quart white wine
juice of 1 lemon
1 cup vodka
2 cups water OR
    2 cups seltzer (club soda)

Marinate crushed oranges and sugar overnight. Combine with the other ingredients and serve in tall glasses. Serves 4.

Cucumber Punch
Poncz Ogórkowy

4 cucumbers
4 lemons
2 cups sugar
1 fifth sauternes (or other white wine)
1 fifth vodka
10 egg whites

Purée the cucumbers if you own a blender; or, pare, grate and press through a sieve. Blend well with all the other ingredients except the egg whites. Beat the whites until they form peaks, then fold into cucumber mixture. Serve in iced glasses on a hot afternoon.

White Wine Punch
Poncz na Białym Winie

juice of 2 lemons
grated rinds of 2 lemons
juice of 3 oranges
grated rinds of 3 oranges
1 cup water
3 cups sugar
1 quart white wine
1 cup vodka

Combine the first 6 ingredients and bring to a boil. Add the wine and vodka. Mix well and serve in punch cups, warm, on a wintry evening.

Chocolate Liqueur
Likier Czekoladowy

6 egg yolks
1 cup sugar
3 ounces baking chocolate
4 tablespoons light cream
2 cups vodka
½ cup whipping cream, whipped

Combine yolks and sugar. Whip until frothy. Heat the chocolate and light cream in the top of a double boiler until melted, then combine with the egg mixture and the vodka. Pour into glasses and top with the whipped cream. Excellent after dinner!

Honeyed Vodka
Miodówka

2 cups sugar
½ cup boiled water
2 cups boiled water
1 cinnamon stick
10 whole cloves
2 teaspoons whole allspice berries OR
    1 teaspoon ground allspice
1 tablespoon anise seeds
2 cups honey
2 cups vodka

Combine sugar and ½ cup water over medium heat, stirring constantly until carmelized. Slowly add the remaining 2 cups of water and spices. Heat for 10 minutes, then strain through cheesecloth. Stir in honey, bring just to a boil, then remove from heat. Combine honey mixture with vodka, stirring constantly, and serve hot.

New Year's Eve Punch
Poncz Noworoczny

5 oranges (the juice and strips of rind)
5 lemons (the juice and strips of rind)
1 pound sugar
1 fifth sauternes (or other white wine)
1 fifth vodka

Juice the oranges and lemons. Slice the rinds into segments and remove membranes. Combine all ingredients and heat through, but do not boil. Remove rinds and serve immediately.

Honeyed Punch
Poncz Miodowy

3 egg yolks
1 cup honey
juice of 2 lemons
6 slices lemon rind
2 cups hot, strong tea
1 cup vodka

Combine egg yolks with the honey. Gradually stir in the strong tea, juice and lemon rind. At the last minute add the vodka. Serve immediately. (Terrific in combatting a cold or the flu!)

At Easter the dinner table is decorated with bottles of vodka and liqueurs that are flavored at home and tinted in colors of gold, green and red. Egg liqueur is a favorite flavor at this time of year.

Egg Liqueur
Likier z Jajkami

2 cups sugar
6 egg yolks
1 cup scalded milk
1 teaspoon vanilla extract
2 cups vodka
½ cup cognac

Combine sugar and eggs. Whip until frothy. Add other ingredients and beat thoroughly. Allow flavors to blend for 2 days in the refrigerator. Tint with food color if desired. Serve chilled and well shaken.

Hot Mead with Vodka
Krupnik

2 cups honey
1 cup water
7 whole cloves
12 cinnamon sticks
½ teaspoon nutmeg
½ vanilla bean OR
   2 teaspoons vanilla extract
2 strips lemon rind
1 fifth vodka

Combine and heat the honey and water. Slip all spices into a cheesecloth sack and add to the honey mixture. Bring to a boil, then remove from heat and allow flavors to blend for an hour or more. Remove spice sack. Heat again—do not boil—and mix well with the vodka. Serve each cup with a cinnamon stick for a stirrer.

Note: This mead mixture may be made ahead of time, then warmed up just before serving. This is a time-honored hot beverage that is still a favorite on a cold day.

Lemon and Milk Vodka

Cytrynówka z Mlekiem

1 whole lemon, halved and seeds removed
1 vanilla bean, sliced lengthwise
1 quart milk
1 cup sugar
2 cups vodka

Place lemon and vanilla bean halves in a sterilized 2-quart jar. Scald milk, then dissolve the sugar in the hot milk. Cool, add to the lemon/vanilla mixture. Finally add the vodka. Cork and place the bottle in the refrigerator for 2 or 3 days. At that time, filter the mixture through cheesecloth and pour into another clean bottle. Seal. Serve chilled.

Vanilla Vodka

Waniliówka

3 vanilla beans
1 cup vodka
1 quart water, boiled
3 pounds sugar
1 quart vodka

Slice vanilla beans and combine with one cup vodka. Pour into a sterilized bottle, seal and store in a dark, cool place for 10 days. At that time, boil the water and sugar to form a syrup. Cool slightly, then combine with the vanilla mixture and the remaining quart of vodka. Strain, then pour into other sterilized bottles. Seal, and age for several months.

Angelica Vodka
Angelika

¼ *cup angelica seeds*
½ *tablespoon fennel seeds*
½ *tablespoon coriander seeds*
½ *tablespoon anise seeds*
1 *quart vodka*
2 *cups boiled water*
2 *cups sugar*

Crush seeds and spices with a rolling pin. Combine with vodka in a sterilized jar or bottle, seal and let flavors blend for a week in a cool place. At that time, boil the water and sugar to form a syrup. Strain the vodka mixture through cheesecloth and slowly combine with the syrup. Pour into sterilized bottles, seal and store for 6 weeks to age.

Herb Vodka
Ziołówka

½ *quart water, boiled*
1 *pound sugar*
⅓ *cup lemon juice*
¼ *cup thinly sliced lemon peels*
1 *tablespoon angelica root*
1 *tablespoon coriander*
pinch anise seeds
½ *quart vodka*

Combine all ingredients except vodka and bring to a boil. Cool, add vodka, pour into sterilized bottle and seal. After a month of setting in a dark place, filter the brew through cheesecloth, and pour into another clean bottle and cap.

Caraway Seed Vodka
Kminkówka

½ cup boiled, chilled water
4 cups vodka
4 tablespoons caraway seeds
3½ cups water, boiled
1 cup sugar

Combine the first 3 ingredients in sterilized bottle; cork it and let set for 4 days. Combine water and sugar and heat until syrupy. Filter the caraway-vodka mixture through cheesecloth, add to the hot syrup, and pour into another clean bottle. Cap it. Chill and serve. Keep refrigerated.

Caraway seeds are reputed to aid in the digestion of starchy foods such as potatoes or cabbage. Possibly its delightful flavor isn't the only reason caraway is such a popular ingredient in Polish recipes.

Vodka with Orange
Wódka Pomarańczowa

1 fifth vodka
orange rind, cut into slivers, membrane removed
1 teaspoon sugar

Combine ingredients; allow to blend for 3 days in refrigerator. Remove rind and serve chilled. Straining through a cheesecloth creates the most clear beverage. (Be sure to wring out every last drop!)

Tangerine Vodka
Mandarynówka

4 tangerines
1 quart vodka
4 cups water
4 cups sugar

Peel tangerines, removing white membrane. Slice peelings into slim strips. Squeeze out the juice; discard seeds and pulp. Combine juice, peelings, and vodka. Pour into a sterilized bottle; seal, and let flavors blend overnight. Boil the water and sugar to form a syrup, cool slightly, then combine slowly with the vodka mixture. Strain and pour into sterilized bottles, seal, and store for several months in a dark, cool place to age.

Vodka with Lemon
Wódka Cytrynowa

1 fifth vodka
lemon rind, cut into thin slivers, membrane removed
1 teaspoon sugar

Combine ingredients; allow to blend in refrigerator for 3 days. Remove rind and serve chilled.

Easy Lemon Vodka
Lekka Cytrynówka

Put the peelings of 1 lemon (white membranes removed) into a pint of vodka. Remove the peelings after 5 hours.

Vodka with Prunes
Śliwowica

2 cups chopped, pitted prunes
1 cup boiling water
1 fifth vodka

Combine the prunes and boiling water in a sterilized jar. Add the vodka, seal, allow to blend for 2 months in a cool place. Turn the bottle every other day. At the end of 2 months, strain, and serve chilled.

Easy Tea Flavored Vodka
Lekka Wódka Herbaciana

Place a pint of vodka and an ordinary tea bag in a large-mouthed vessel. After 2 or 3 hours remove tea bag.

Fast Cherry Vodka
Lekka Wiśniówka

Combine 1 cup of cherries (halved and pitted) with a pint of vodka for 3 to 4 hours. Strain through cheesecloth and serve.

Quick Cherry Pit Vodka
Wódka z Pestek Czereśniowych

Crush ¼ cup cherry stones and combine with a pint of vodka. Allow flavors to blend overnight before straining through cheesecloth.

Wild Strawberry Cordial
Likier Poziomkowy

2½ pounds cleaned, stemmed strawberries
1 quart vodka
2 cups sugar

Combine strawberries and vodka in a large, sterilized container. Seal and set in a dark, cool place for a week. At that time, pour the strawberry-flavored vodka into sterilized bottles, and seal. To the remaining strawberries, add the sugar. Mix well then seal and place the vodka bottles and the berry-mix container in a cool, dark place for a month.

After a month has elapsed, combine the berry mixture with the vodka, strain, and pour into fresh, sterilized bottles. Seal and allow to age for several months in a cool, dark place. It's worth the wait!

Fresh raspberries may be substituted for the strawberries, in which case, the Polish name would be *Likier Malinowy*. A substitution of peaches (2½ pounds peeled, sliced and pitted) would be *Likier Brzoskwiniowy*. Pitted Apricot Cordial, using 2½ pounds of peeled, sliced and pitted apricots, would be called, *Likier z Drelowanych Moreli*.

Buffalo-Grass Vodka
Żubrówka

Place several blades of the buffalo grass into a pint of vodka. After 6 hours remove the grass.

Anise Flavored Vodka
Anyszówka

Combine 1 pint vodka with ½ teaspoon anise seeds. Allow flavors to blend for about 3 hours, then strain through cheesecloth.

Peppery Vodka
Pieprzówka

To a pint of vodka add 1 tablespoon whole peppercorns. After 2 or 3 hours strain through cheesecloth.

Index

Almond
  Baba, 23, 26
  Butter Cookies, 119, 123
  Christmas Soup, 147, 148
  Honey — Cookies, 157, 161
Angelica Vodka, 188
Angelika, 188
Anise Flavored Vodka, 193
Anyszówka, 193
Apple(s)
  /Beet/Cabbage Salad, 171, 172
  in Creamy Beet Glaze, 23, 24
  Crêpes with — Filling, 130-131
  Crunchy — Carrot Salad, 176
  Cucumber — Salad, 138
  Hot Beet and Ripe — Relish,
    126
  Orange Glazed, 174
  Raisin Cake, 115, 118
  Roast Pork with — Juice
    Glaze, 131
  Tangy — and Leek Salad, 86
  Veal Simmered with, 57
Apricot, Chilled Soup, 132
Artichoke, Frosty Salad, 79, 80

Asparagus, 9, 23
  au Gratin, 23, 26
  Fresh — Omelet, 96, 97
  Steamed Tips, 145

Baba
  Almond, 23, 26
  Easter, 67
  Icing, 67
Babeczki w Fartuszkach
  Papierowych, 95, 98
Babka Migdalowa, 23, 26
Babka Wielkanocna, 61, 67
Baby Carrots Polonaise, 33, 37,
  147, 152
Bacon
  Bisque of Potato with, 158
  Potatoes with — Bits, 127, 128
  Raw Spinach and — Salad,
    134
Baked Ham, 61, 64
Baked Omelet with Wine Sauce
  75, 76-77
Baked Polish Ham, 171, 173

195

Baked Potato with Mushroom
 Topping, 49, 52
Baranie Ptaszki, 75, 78
Barshch
 Christmas Eve Barszcz, 148
 Easy, 11, 16
 Hot Beer, 11, 18
Barszcz Czerwony, 11, 16-17
Barszcz Wigilijny, 147, 148
Barszcz Wiosenny, 11, 12
Basic Beef Broth, 11, 17
Basil, 169
Bechamel Sauce, 23, 25, 160
Beef
 Basic Broth, 11, 17
 Grilled Tenderloin with
  Mushroom Caps, 139
Beer
 Hot Beer Barshch, 11, 18
 Hot Soup, 11, 18-19
 Soup with Eggs, 147, 149
Beetroot Soup, 11, 16-17
Beet(s)
 Apple/ — /Cabbage Salad, 172
 Apples in Creamy — Glaze,
  23, 24
 Clear Soup, 11, 14
 Cold Soup with Beet Greens,
  11, 15
 Easy Barshch, 11, 16
 and Horseradish Relish, 62
 Hot Beer Harshch, 11, 18
 Soup, 11, 13
 Spring Barshch, 11, 12
Bisque of Potato Soup with
 Bacon, 157, 158
Blueberry, Chilled Soup, 83
Boiled Crayfish, 61, 63
Bomba Owocowa, 49, 52-53
Braised Carrots, 55, 58
Braised Liver with Bacon, 33, 35
Braised Spring Lamb with
 Cabbage, 49, 51
Brandied Peaches, 143, 146
Bread, 44
 Buttered Crumbs, 37
 Christmas Eve, 153-154

Freshly Baked Potato, 28-29
Poppyseed Roll, 154-155
Potato Round, 82
Pudding Topped with
 Whipped Sour Cream, 137,
 140
Rye, 122
Toasted Triangles, 50
Brukselka w Bialym Sosie z Serem,
 137, 139-140
Brussels Sprouts in Light Cheese
 Sauce, 137, 139-140
*Brzoskwinie i Sliwki w Muszelkach z
 Ciasta*, 89, 93-94
Brzoskwinie Zapawiane Gorzalką,
 143, 146
Buckwheat Groats, 55, 57-58
Budyń z Ryżu z Bitą Smietaną, 109,
 112-113
Buffalo Grass Vodka, 182
Bulls Eye Eggs, 33, 34-35
Buleczki z Makiem, 23
Buraczki z Jablkami na Gorąco, 125,
 126
Buttered Baby Carrots, 129, 131
Buttered Bread Crumbs, 37

Cabbage, 19
 Apple/Beet Salad, 172
 Braised Spring Lamb with, 51
 Leek and Orange Salad, 157,
  158
 Roast Duck Served with Red,
  164-165
 Roll-Ups, 175, 176-177
 Savoy Polonaise, 27, 30-31
 Stuffed Pierogi, 33, 35-36
Candied Orange Peel, 69
Caraway Seed Vodka, 189
Carp with Horseradish Sauce,
 147, 151
Carrots
 Baby, Polonaise, 37, 152
 Braised, 58
 Buttered Baby, 131

Crunchy Apple Salad, 176
Succulent Rhubarb and, 50
Cauliflower
  Cream of — Soup, 77-78
  Flounder with, 97
  Green Pepper and, 110
Caviar, 179
Celery
  Fresh — Root Salad, 34
  Vinegar I, 33, 34
  Vinegar II, 44
Cheesecake, 133, 136
Cherry Dumplings, 171, 173
Chestnut Stuffing, 61, 66
Chicken, 9
  Homemade Stock, 11, 13
  Livers Simmered in Madeira
    Sauce, 143, 145
  Paprika, 11, 20
Chicory, Hot Polish, 152
Chilled Apricot Soup, 129, 132
Chilled Blueberry Soup, 79, 83
Chilled Eggs and Medley of
  Fresh Vegetables, 163, 164
Chleb Wigilijny, 147, 153-154
Chlebowy Budyń z Bitą Smietaną,
  137, 140
Chlodnik Borówkowy, 79, 83
Chlodnik Brzoskwiniowy, 129, 132
Christmas
  Almond Soup, 147, 148
  Eve Barszcz, 147, 148
  Eve Bread, 147, 153-154
Chocolate Liqueur, 183
  Mazurek, 125, 128
*Chrupiąca Salatka z Jablek i
  Marchewki*, 175, 176
Chrusty, 33, 38-39
Ciastka Migdalowe na Maśle, 119,
  123
Cielęcina Duszona z Jablkami, 55,
  57
Cielęcina Marynowana, 79, 81
Cienka Zupa Buraczana, 11, 14
Clear Beet Soup, 11, 14
Coddled Fish Fillets in Shrimp
  Sauce, 41, 45

Cold Beet Soup with Beet
  Greens, 11, 15
Cottage Style Eggs and Potatoes,
  133, 135
Court Bouillon, 150
Cracklings, 33, 37-39
Crayfish, 45
  Boiled, 63
  Shrimp or — Stuffing, 65
Cream of Cauliflower Soup with
  Buttered Croutons, 75, 77-78
Cream Puff Pie, 175, 178
Creamed Spinach, 99, 101
Crêpes
  with Apple Filling, 129,
    130-131
  with Mushroom Filling, 143,
    144
  à la Polonaise, 85, 87
Crunchy Apple Carrot Salad,
  175, 176
Cucumber
  Apple Salad, 137, 138
  Punch, 182
Cucumbers in Sour Cream
  Relish, 175, 176
Ćwikla z Chrzanem, 61, 62
Cytrynówka z Miekiem, 187

Date Mazurek, 61
  I, 68-69
  II, 70
Deviled Eggs with Mushroom
  Bits, 137, 138
Dill Butter, 93
Dill, fresh, 7
Dolki z Ostrygami, 89, 90-91
Duck, Roast Served with Red
  Cabbage, 164-165
Dumplings
  Cherry, 173
  New Potato, 11
Duszone Koniuszki Szparagowe,
  143, 145
Duszone Ziemniaki, 163
Dutch Oven Braised Ham, 23, 24

Easter, 61, 185
  Baba, 61, 67
Easy
  Barshch, 11, 16
  Lemon Vodka, 190
  Pastry Dough, 159
  Tea Flavored Vodka, 191
Egg(s)
  Baked with Bechamel Sauce,
    157, 160
  Baked Omelet with Wine
    Sauce, 76, 77
  Baked in Sea Shells, 125, 126
  with Bechamel Sauce, 23, 25
  Bulls Eye, 34-35
  Chilled — and Medley of
    Fresh Vegetables, 164
  Cottage Style and Potatoes,
    135
  with Cream in Ramekins, 55,
    56
  Deviled with Mushroom Bits,
    138
  Fresh Asparagus Omelet,
    96-97
  and Ham Roll-Ups, 103, 104
  Hard-cooked Easter, 61
  Hard-cooked Flowerettes, 43
  Layered — and Vegetable
    Casserole, 168-169
  Lettuce and Sliced — Salad,
    11, 19
  Liqueur, 185
  Mushroom Omelet Torte, 100
  Pickled, 120
  à la Polonaise, 49, 50
  Scrambled, Sprinkled with
    Chives, 117
  "in the Shell," 109, 110
  Shirred, 172
  Smoked Salmon Omelets, 149
  Sunny Side Up, 27
Eggplant Crisps, 175, 177
Endive with Fresh Mayonnaise,
  41, 43
Endywia z Majonezem. 41, 43
Escarole, 130

Fast Cherry Vodka, 191
Faszerowane Jajka z Grzybami, 137
  138
Fish
  Carp with Horseradish Sauce,
    151
  Coddled Fillets in Shrimp
    Sauce, 45
  Flounder with Cauliflower, 97
  Poached Pike, 150
Flądra z Kalafiolem, 95, 97
Flybanes, 79, 80
Flounder with Cauliflower, 95,
  97
Fresh Asparagus Omelet, 95,
  96-97
Fresh Celery Root Salad, 33, 34
Fresh Green Peas, 133
  with Dill Butter, 89, 92-93
  with Tiny Onion Rings, 109,
    112
Fresh Seasonal Fruit Tray, 75
Freshly Baked Potato Bread, 27
  28-29
Frosty Artichoke Salad, 79, 80
Fruit Bombe, 49, 53
Fruit Compote, 147, 155
Fruit Cream with Wine, 41, 47

Galareta z Lodów Waniliwych, 167
  170
Gęsta Potrawka Myśliwska, 119,
  121
Gęsta Zupa Kartoflana z Wędzonką,
  157, 158
Gołąbki Mięsne z Ryżem, 175,
  176-177
Goose, Savory Wild, 111
Gorący Barszcz na Piwie, 11, 18
Gotowany Szczupak na Gorąco,
  147, 150
Gorące Bułeczki z Masłem, 95
Green Pepper and Cauliflower
  Toss, 109, 110
Grilled Tenderloin with
  Mushroom Caps, 137, 139
Grilled Tomatoes, 115, 117

Groszek z Masłem Koperkowym, 89, 92-93
Groszek z Pierścieniami Drobnej Cebuli, 109, 112
Grzyby Marynowane, 89, 90
Guinea Hen, Roasted, 86
Gypsy Mazur, 61, 72

Ham, 23
  Baked, 64
  Baked Polish, 173
  Dutch Oven Braised, 23, 24
  Egg and — Roll-Ups, 104
  Hard-cooked Easter Eggs, 61
Egg Flowerettes, 41, 43
Herb Vodka, 188
Herbed Tomato Salad, 95, 96
Homemade Chicken Stock, 11, 13
Homemade Kielbasa, 27, 30
Honey Almond Cookies, 157, 161
Honeyed Punch, 185
Honeyed Vodka, 184
Horseradish Sauce, 61, 63
Hot Beer Barshch, 11, 18
Hot Beer Soup, 11, 18-19
Hot Beet and Ripe Apple Relish, 125, 126
Hot Mead with Vodka, 186
Hot Polish Chicory, 147, 152
Hunters' Stew, 119, 121

Ice Cream, Vanilla, 123
Iced Coffee Polish Style, 181
  with Vodka, 181
Individual Oyster Soufflés, 89, 90-91
Indyk w Przyprawie Majonezowej, 103, 104-105

Jabłka w Glazurze Baruczanej, 23, 24
Jagnię w Kapuście, 49, 51
Jaja Sadzone w Białym Sosie, 23, 25-26

Jaja na Śmietanie w Miseczce, 55, 56
Jajecznica ze Szczypiórkiem, 115 117
Jajka Faszerowane, 109, 110
Jabłka w Glazurze Pomarańczowe 171, 174
Jajka z Kartoflami po Wiejsku, 133 135
Jajka Pieczone w Muszelkach Morskich, 125, 126
Jajka a la Polonaise, 49, 50
Jajka Wielkanocnena Twardo, 61
Jajka Wypiekane w Białym Sosie, 157, 160
Jajka Wypiekane w Śmietanie, 171, 172
Jajka Zapiekane z Jarzyną, 167, 168-169
Jelenie Bitki w Sosie Winnym, 133, 135

Kapusta Włoska po Polsku, 27, 30-31
Karp w Sosie Chrzanowym, 147, 151
Kartofle z Posiekaną Wędzonką, 125, 127-128
Kartofle Wypiekane z Grzybami, 49, 52
Kasza Gryczana, 55, 57-58
Kawa Mrożona po Polsku, 181
Kawa Mrożona z Wódką, 181
Kielbasa, 27, 29
  Homemade, 27, 30
Kielbasa, 27, 29
Kielbasa Domowa, 27, 30
Kielbasa Polska, 61
King Boreas, 107
Kminkówka, 189
Knedelki z Kartofli, 11, 20
Knedle z Kartofli Duszonych i Mąki, 115, 118
Knedle Wiśniowe, 171, 173
Kompot Letni, 85, 86
Kompot Owocowy, 147, 155

Kotlety Wieprzowe, Duszone w Czerwonym Winie, 167, 169
Krokiety z Jajek i Szynki, 103, 104
Kruchy Placek z Bakłażanów, 175, 177
Krupnik, 186

Lamb, 9
    Birds, 75, 78
    Braised Spring with Cabbage, 51
Layered Egg and Vegetable Casserole, 167, 168-169
Leek, Cabbage and Orange Salad, 158
Lekki Barszcz, 11, 16
Lekka Cytrynówka, 190
Lekka Wiśniówka, 191
Lekka Wódka Herbaciana, 191
Lemon juice, 19
Lemon and Milk Vodka, 187
Lettuce and Sliced Egg Salad, 11, 19
Likier Brzoskwiniowy, 192
Likier Czekoladowy, 183
Likier Drelowanych Moreli, 192
Likier z Jajkami, 185
Likier Malinowy, 192
Likier Poziomkowy, 192
Liver, Braised with Bacon, 35
Lody, 119
Lukrowa Babka, 67

Madeleines, 95, 98
Makownik Zawijany, 147, 154-155
Mandarynówka, 190
Marchewka Duszona, 55, 58
Marchewka na Maśle, 129, 131
Marchewka po Polsku, 147, 152
Marinated Veal, 79, 81
Mashed Potatoes, 163
Mayonnaise (Blender Method), 105
Mazurek
    [Mazurka] Royale, 21

Date I, 68-69
Date II, 70
Orange, 70-71
Raisin, 71
Gypsy [Mazur], 72
Mazurek Cygański, 61, 72
Mazurek Czekoladowy, 125, 128
Mazurek Daktylowy, 61, 68-69, 70
Mazurek Pomarańczowy, 61, 70-71
Mazurek z Rodzynkami, 61, 71
Mazurka Royale, 9, 11, 21
Meringue, 59
Miniature Meat Patties, 157, 159
Miodówka, 184
Mizeria z Ogórków i Jabłek, 137, 138
Młoda Marchewka po Polsku, 33, 37
Mrożonka z Truskawek, 99, 102
Muchomory, 79, 80
Mushrooms
    Baked Potato with — Topping, 52
    Crêpes with — Filling, 144
    Deviled Eggs with — Bits, 138
    Filling, 144
    Grilled Tenderloin with — Caps, 139
    Omelet Torte, 99, 100
    Pickled, 90
    Stuffed Tomatoes, 147, 153
Muzurek Królewski, 11, 21

Nadzienie z Maronów, 61, 66
Nadzienie z Raczków, 61, 65
Nadzienie z Rodzynkami, 61, 65-66, 89, 92
Naleśniki z Nadzieniem Grzybowym, 143, 144
Naleśniki Nadziewane Jabłkami, 129, 130-131
New Potato Dumplings, 11, 20
New Year's Eve Punch, 184

Ocet Selerowy, 33, 34
Ogórki z Cebulą w Śmietanie na Liściach Szpinakowych, 41, 42

Ogórki w Przyprawie z Kwaśne Śmietany, 175, 176
Okągly Chleb Kartoflany, 79, 82
Omelet(s)
  Baked with Wine Sauce, 76, 77
  Mushroom Torte, 100
  Smoked Salmon, 149
Omelet ze Świeżych Szparagów, 95, 96-97
Omelety z Wędzonym Łososiem, 147, 149
Omlety Wypiekane w Sosie Winnym, 75, 76-77
Onion, 7, 19
  Fresh Peas with Tiny — Rings, 112
  Sour Cream Cucumbers and — Rings Arranged on Crisp Spinach Leaves, 42
Orange
  Butter Cake, 163, 165
  Cabbage, Leek and — Salad, 158
  Glazed Apples, 174
  Mazurek, 61, 70-71
Oysters, Individual Soufflés, 90-91

Paprykarz z Kury, 11, 20
Parsley, 97
Pastry Dough, 159
Peach(es)
  Brandied, 146
  Tarts, 89, 93-94
Peas
  Fresh with Dill Butter, 92-93
  Fresh Green, 133
  Fresh with Tiny Onion Rings, 112
  and Ripe Tomato Salad, 55, 56
Peppery Vodka, 193
Pickled Eggs, 120
Pickled Mushrooms, 89, 90
Pieczeń Wieprzowa z Glazurą Jablecznikową, 129, 131
Pieczona Kaczka z Czerwoną Kapustą, 163, 164-165

Pieczona Panterka, 85, 87
Pieczone Pomidory, 115, 117
Pieczony Indyk, 61, 64-65
Pieczony Prosiak, 89, 91
Pieprzówka, 193
Pierniczki z Migdalami, 157, 161
Pierożki z Kapusty, 33, 35-36
Pig, Roast Suckling, 91
Pikantna Salatka z Jablek i Porów, 85, 86
Piwna Zupa z Jajkami, 147, 149
Placek z Jabtkowy z Rodzynkami, 115, 118
Placek z Kwaśnej Śmietany i Zóltek pod Pianą z Bialek, 175, 178
Placek Omeletowy z Grzybami, 99, 100
Placek z Orzechów Wloskich, 103, 106
Placki Kartoflane, 41, 46-47, 99, 101
Plum Tarts, 89, 93
Poached Pike, 147, 150
Polędwica z Pieczarkami, 137, 139
Polish Sausage, 61
  Simmered in Wine, 115, 116
Polska Cykoria na Gorąco, 147, 150
Polska Kielbasa Grzana w Winie, 115, 116
Polskie Naleśniki, 85, 87
Polska Szynka Pieczona, 171, 173
Pomarańczowy Placek na Másle, 163, 165
Pomidory Nadziewane Grzybami, 147, 153
Poncz na Bialym Winie, 183
Poncz Letni, 182
Poncz Miodowy, 185
Poncz Noworoczny, 184
Poncz Ogórkowy, 182
Poppyseed Roll, 147, 154-155
Pork
  Miniature Meat Patties, 159
  Ribs and Cabbage, 125, 127
  Roast with Apple Juice Glaze, 131
  Roast Suckling Pig, 91

Steaks Simmered in Red Wine Sauce, 167, 169
Potato(es)
  with Bacon Bits, 125, 127-128
  Baked with Mushroom Topping, 52
  Bisque of with Bacon, 158
  Cottage Style Eggs and, 135
  Crouquettes, 115, 118
  Mashed, 163
  New — Dumplings, 11, 20
  Pancakes, 41, 46
  Pancakes II, 99, 101
  Round Bread, 79, 82
  Salad, 61, 62
Potrawka Letnia, 99, 100
Poziomki z Bitą Smietaną, 27, 31
Przetarte Owoce z Winem, 41, 47
Przypiekane Polowki Chleba, 49, 50
Punch
  Cucumber, 182
  Honeyed, 185
  New Year's Eve, 184
  Summer, 182
  White Wine, 183

Quick Cherry Pit Vodka, 191

Radish/Escarole Bowl, 129, 130
Raisin Mazurek, 61, 71
Raisin Stuffing, 61
  I, 65-66
  II, 89, 92
Raki Gotowane, 61, 63
Raw Spinach and Bacon Salad, 133, 134
Raw Spinach and Pickled Egg Salad, 119, 120
Rhubarb, 9
  Succulent — and Carrot Relish, 50
Rice Pudding Garnished with Sour Cream Topping, 109, 112-113
Roast Duck Served with Red Cabbage, 163, 164-165

Roast Pork with Apple Juice Glaze, 129, 131
Roast Suckling Pig, 89, 91
Roast Turkey, 61, 64-65
Roasted Guinea Hen, 85, 96
Rosól Domowy z Kury, 11, 13
Rosól Wolowy, 11, 17
Różyczki z Jajek, 41, 43
Ryba Duszona w Sosie Rakowym, 41, 45
Rye Bread with Sweet Butter, 119, 122

Sadzone Oczká z Jajek, 27
Salads
  Apple/Beet/Cabbage, 172
  Cabbage, Leek and Orange, 158
  Crunchy Apple Carrot, 176
  Cucumber Apple, 138
  Endive with Fresh Mayonnaise, 43
  Frosty Artichoke, 80
  Green Pepper and Cauliflower Toss, 110
  Hard-cooked Egg Flowerettes, 43
  Herbed Tomato, 96
  Lettuce and Sliced Egg, 9
  Peas and Ripe Tomato, 56
  Potato, 62
  Radish/Escarole Bowl, 130
  Raw Spinach and Bacon, 134
  Raw Spinach and Pickled Egg, 120
  September, 116
  Sour Cream Cucumbers and Onion Rings Arranged on Crisp Spinach Leaves, 42
  Succulent Rhubarb and Carrot Relish, 50
  Summer, 76
  Tangy Apple and Leek, 86
  Winter's Seasonal, 168
Salata z Jajkami, 11, 19
Salata z Kapusty, Porów i Pomaranczy, 157, 158

Salata na Sezon Zimowy, 167, 168
Salata Wloska z Rzodkiewka, 129, 130
Salata Wrześniowa, 115, 116
Salata z Zielonych Artyczoków z Majonezem, 79, 80
Salata z Ziemniaków, 61, 62
Salata z Groszku i Świeżych Pomidorów, 55, 56
Salatka z Jajek, Buraków i Kapusty, 171, 172
Salatka Pomidorowa z Ziolami, 95, 96
Salatka z Korzeni Selerowych, 33, 34
Salatka Letnia, 75, 76
Salatka z Papryki i Kalafiorów, 109, 110
Salatka ze Swieżego Szpinaku z Wędzonką, 133, 134
Salatka ze Szpinaku z Kiszonymi Jajkami, 119, 120
Sauces
  Bechamel, 25, 160
  Dill Butter, 93
  Horseradish, 63, 151
  Mayonnaise (Blender Method), 105
  Sweet/Sour Dressing, 134
  Wine, 77
Sauerkraut, 19
Sausages, 27
  Kielbasa, 29
  Homemade, 30
  Polish, 61
  Simmered in Wine, 116
Savoy Cabbage Polonaise, 27, 30-31
Savory Wild Goose, 109, 111
Scrambled Eggs Sprinkled with Chives, 115, 117
September Salad, 115, 116
Sernik, 133, 136
Shrimp
  (or Crayfish) Stuffing, 61, 65
  Coddled Fish Fillets in — Sauce, 45

Shirred Eggs, 171, 172
Smaczna Gęś Dzika, 109, 111
Smoked Salmon Omelets, 147, 149
Soczysta Salatka z Rabarbaru i Marchewki, 49, 50
Sos Chrzanowy, 61, 63
Soups
  Basic Beef Broth, 11, 17
  Beer with Eggs, 149
  Beet Soup, 11, 13
  Beetroot Soup, 11, 16-17
  Bisque of Potato with Bacon, 158
  Chilled Apricot, 132
  Chilled Blueberry, 83
  Christmas Almond, 148
  Christmas Eve Barszcz, 148
  Clear Beet Soup, 11, 14
  Cold Beet Soup with Beet Greens, 11, 15
  Cream of Cauliflower, 77-78
  Easy Barshch, 11, 16
  Homemade Chicken Stock 11, 13
  Hot Beer Barshch, 11, 18
  Hot Beer Soup, 11, 18-19
  Spring Barshch, 11, 12
  Summer's Potage, 100
Sour cream, 12, 19
  Cucumbers and Onion Rings Arranged on Crisp Spinach Leaves, 41, 42
  Cucumber in Relish, 176
  Rice Pudding Garnished with — Topping, 112-113
  Whipped, 31, 140
Special Soup Recipes, 11
Spinach
  Creamed, 101
  Raw — and Bacon Salad, 134
  Raw — and Pickled Egg Salad, 120
  Sour Cream Cucumbers and Onion Rings Arranged on Crisp Leaves, 42
Spring Barshch, 11, 12

Spring Cream Cheese Spread,
27, 28
Strawberries, 9
Mousse, 99, 102
Tarts, 55, 58-59
Wild — Cordial, 192
Wild with Whipped Sour
Cream, 27, 31
Steamed Asparagus Tips, 143,
145
Succulent Rhubarb and Carrot
Relish, 49, 50
Summer Compote, 85, 86
Summer Punch, 182
Summer Salad, 75, 76
Summer's Potage, 99, 100
Sweet/Sour Dressing, 134
Sznycelki w Cieście, 157, 159
Szynka Duszona w Rondlu, 23, 24
Szynka Pieczona, 61, 64
*Szparagi Wypiekane z Tarta
Buleczką*, 23, 26
Szpinak Przecierany, 99, 101
Śliwowica, 191
Świeży Chleb Kartoflany, 27, 28-29
Świeży Groszek Zielony, 133

Taca Świeżych Owoców, 75
Tangerine Vodka, 190
Tangy Apple and Leek Salad,
85, 86
Toasted Bread Triangles, 49, 50
Tomatoes
Grilled, 117
Herbed Salad, 96
Mushroom Stuffed, 153
Peas and Ripe — Salad, 56
Traditional Pastry Dough, 159
Truskawki w Muszelkach z Ciasta,
55, 58-59
Turkey
Platter with Mayonnaise
Garnish, 103, 104-105
Roast, 64, 65

Vanilla Cream Mold, 167, 170
Vanilla Ice Cream, 119, 123
Vanilla Sugar, 31
Vanilla Vodka, 187
Veal
Marinated, 81
Simmered with Apples, 55, 57
Venison Steaks in Wine Sauce,
133, 135
Vodka
Angelica, 188
Anise Flavored, 193
Buffalo Grass, 192
Caraway Seed, 189
Easy Lemon, 190
Easy Tea Flavored, 191
Fast Cherry, 191
Herb, 188
Honeyed, 185
Hot Mead with, 186
with Lemon, 190
Lemon and Milk, 187
with Orange, 189
Peppery, 193
with Prunes, 191
Quick Cherry Pit, 191
Tangerine, 190
Vanilla, 187

Walnut Torte, 103, 106
Waniliówka, 187
Wątróbka Duszona z Wędzonką, 33,
35
*Wątróbka Kurza Duszona w Sosie
Madejra*, 143, 145
Whipped Sour Cream, 137, 140
White Icing, 128
White Wine Punch, 183
Wigilijna Zupa Migdalowa, 147,
148
Wild Strawberries with
Whipped Sour Cream, 27, 31
Wild Strawberry Cordial, 192
Wine Sauce, 77
Winter's Seasonal Salad, 167,
168

Wiosenna Przyprawa z Sera Smietankowego, 27, 28
Wole Oczka z Jajek, 33, 34-35
Wódka Cytrynowa, 190
Wódka z Pestek Czereśniowych, 191
Wódka Pomarańczowa, 189

Zimne Jajka i Wybór Jarzyn Świeżych, 163, 164
Ziolówka, 188

Zupa Buraczana, 11, 13-14
Zupa Kalafiorowa z Grzankami, 75, 77-78
Zupa z Liści Burakowych na Zimno, 11, 15
Zupa z Piwa na Gorąco, 11, 18
Żeberka Wieprzowe z Kapustą, 125, 127
Żubrówka, 192
Żytni Chleb na Słodkim Maśle, 119, 122